W9-APX-653

No Late Check-out!

FRONT DESK

KELLY YANG

THORNDIKE PRESS
A part of Gale, a Cengage Company

GALE
A Cengage Company

Farmington Hills, Mich • San Francisco • New York • Waterville, Maine
Meriden, Conn • Mason, Ohio • Chicago

ONONDAGA FREE

Recommended for Middle Readers.
Copyright © 2018 by Yang Yang.
Thorndike Press, a part of Gale, a Cengage Company.

Thorndike Press® Large Print Mini-Collections.
The text of this Large Print edition is unabridged.
Other aspects of the book may vary from the original edition.
Set in 16 pt. Plantin.

LIBRARY OF CONGRESS CIP DATA ON FILE.
CATALOGUING IN PUBLICATION FOR THIS BOOK
IS AVAILABLE FROM THE LIBRARY OF CONGRESS

ISBN-13: 978-1-4328-6145-2 (hardcover)

Published in 2018 by arrangement with Scholastic, Inc.

Printed in the United States of America
1 2 3 4 5 6 7 22 21 20 19 18

TO ELIOT, TILDEN, AND NINA,
IN LOVING MEMORY OF
MY LATE GRANDFATHER,
AND TO MY PARENTS,
WHO TAUGHT ME TO DREAM

CHAPTER 1

My parents told me that America would be this amazing place where we could live in a house with a dog, do whatever we want, and eat hamburgers till we were red in the face. So far, the only part of that we've achieved is the hamburger part, but I was still holding out hope. And the hamburgers here are pretty good.

The most incredible burger I've ever had was at the Houston space center last summer. We weren't planning on eating there — everybody knows museum food is fifty thousand times more expensive than outside food. But one whiff of the sizzling bacon as we passed by the café and my knees wobbled. My parents must have heard the howls of my stomach, because the next thing I knew, my mother was rummaging through her purse for coins.

We only had enough money for one hamburger, so we had to share. But, man, what a burger. It was a mile high with real bacon and mayonnaise and pickles!

My mom likes to tease that I devoured the whole thing in one gulp, leaving the two of them only a couple of crumbs. I'd like to think I gave them more than that.

The other thing that was great about that space center was the free air conditioning. We were living in our car that summer, which sounds like a lot of fun but actually wasn't, because our car's AC was busted. So after the burger, my dad parked himself in front of the vent and stayed there the entire rest of the time. It was like he was trying to turn his fingers into Popsicles.

My mom and I bounced from exhibit to exhibit instead. I could barely keep up with her. She was an engineer back in China, so she loves math and rockets. She oohed and aahed over this module and that module. I wished my cousin Shen could have been there. He *loves* rockets too.

When we got to the photo booth, my mother's face lit up. The booth took a picture of you and made it look like you were a real astronaut in space. I went first. I put my head where the cardboard cutout was and smiled when the guy said, *"Cheese."* When it was my mom's turn to take her photo, I thought it would be funny to jump into her shot. The result was a picture of her in an astronaut suit, hovering over Earth, and me standing right next to her in my flip-flops, doing bunny ears with my fingers.

My mother's face crumpled when she saw her picture. She pleaded with the guy to let her take another one, but he said, "No can do. One picture per person." For a second, I thought she was going to cry.

We still have the picture. Every time I look at it, I wish I could go back in time. If I could do it all over again, I would not photobomb my mom's picture. And I'd give her more of my burger. Not the whole thing but definitely some more bites.

At the end of that summer, my dad got a job as an assistant fryer at a Chinese restaurant in California. That meant we didn't have to live in our car anymore and we could move into a small one-bedroom apartment. It also meant my dad brought home fried rice from work every day. But sometimes, he'd also bring back big ol' blisters all up and down his arm. He said they were just allergies. But I didn't think so. I think he got them from frying food all day long in the sizzling wok.

My mom got a job in the front of the

restaurant as a waitress. Everybody liked her, and she got great tips. She even managed to convince the boss to let me go with her to the restaurant after school, since there was nobody to look after me.

My mother's boss was a wrinkly white-haired Chinese man who reeked of garlic and didn't believe in wasting anything — not cooking oil, not toilet paper, and certainly not free labor.

"You think you can handle waitressing, kid?" he asked me.

"Yes, sir!" I said. Excitement pulsated in my ear. My first job! I was determined not to let him down.

There was just one problem — I was only nine then and needed two hands just to hold one dish steady. The other waitresses managed five plates at a time. Some didn't even need hands — they could balance a plate on their shoulder.

When the dinner rush came, I too loaded up my carrying tray with five dishes. Big mistake. As my small back gave in to the mountainous weight, all my dishes came crashing down. Hot soup splashed onto customers, and fried prawns went flying across the restaurant.

I was fired on the spot and so was my mother. No amount of begging or promising to do the dishes for the next gazillion years would change the owner's mind. The whole way home, I fought tears in my eyes.

I thought of my three cousins back home. None of them had ever gotten fired before. Like me, they were only children as well. In China, every child is an only child, ever since the government decided all families are allowed only one. Since none of us had siblings, we were our siblings. Leaving them was the hardest part about leaving China.

I didn't want my mom to see me cry in the car, but eventually that night, she heard me. She came into my room and sat on my bed. "Hey, it's okay," she said in Chinese, hugging me tight. "It's not your fault."

She wiped a tear from my cheek. Through the thin walls, I could hear the sounds of husbands and wives bickering and babies wailing from the neighboring apartments, each one as cramped as ours.

"Mom," I asked her, "why did we come here? Why did we come to America?" I repeated.

My mother looked away and didn't say anything for a long time. A plane flew overhead, and the picture frames on the wall shook.

She looked in my eyes.

"Because it's freer here," she finally said,

which didn't make any sense. Nothing was free in America. Everything was so expensive.

"But, Mom —"

"One day, you'll understand," she said, kissing the top of my head. "Now go to sleep."

I drifted to sleep, thinking about my cousins and missing them and hoping they were missing me back.

After my mother got fired from the restaurant, she got very serious about job hunting. She called it getting back on her horse. It was 1993 and she bought every Chinese newspaper she could find. She pored over the jobs section with a magnifying glass like a scientist. That's when she came across an unusual listing.

A man named Michael Yao had put an ad out in the Chinese newspaper looking for an experienced motel manager. The ad said that he owned a little motel in Anaheim, California, and he was looking for someone to run the place. The job came with free boarding too! My mother jumped up and grabbed the phone — our rent then cost almost all my dad's salary. (And who said things in America were free?)

To her surprise, Mr. Yao was equally

enthusiastic. He didn't seem to mind that my parents weren't experienced and *really* liked the fact that they were a couple.

"Two people for the price of one," he joked in his thick Taiwanese-accented Mandarin when we went over to his house the next day.

My parents smiled nervously while I tried to stay as still as I could and not screw it up for them, like I'd screwed up my mother's restaurant job. We were sitting in the living room of Mr. Yao's house, or rather, his mansion. I made myself look at the floor and not stare at the top of Mr. Yao's head, which was all shiny under the light, like it had been painted in egg white.

The door opened, and a boy about my age walked in. He had on a T-shirt that said *I don't give a,* and underneath it, a picture of a rat and a donkey. I raised an eyebrow.

"Jason," Mr. Yao said to the boy. "Say hello."

"Hi," Jason muttered.

My parents smiled at Jason.

"What grade are you in?" they asked him in Chinese.

Jason replied in English, "I'm going into fifth grade."

"Ah, same as Mia," my mom said. She smiled at Mr. Yao. "Your son's English is so good." She turned to me. "Hear that, Mia? No accent."

My cheeks burned. I felt my tongue in my mouth, like a limp lizard.

"Of course he speaks good English. He was born here," Mr. Yao said. "He speaks *native* English."

Native. I mouthed the word. I wondered if I worked really hard, would I also be able to speak native English one day? Or was that something completely off-limits for me? I looked over at my mom, who was shaking her head. Jason disappeared off to his room, and Mr. Yao asked my parents if they had any questions.

"Just to make sure, we can live at the motel for free?" my mom asked.

"Yes," Mr. Yao said.

"And . . . what about . . ." My mom struggled to get the words out. She shook her head, embarrassed to say it. "Will we get paid?"

"Oh, right, payment," Mr. Yao said, like it hadn't dawned on him at all. "How's five dollars a customer?"

I glanced at my mom. I could tell that she was doing math in her head because she always got this dreamy smile on her face.

"Thirty rooms at five dollars a room — that's a hundred and fifty dollars a night,"

14

my mom said, her eyes widening. She looked at my dad. "That's a lot of money!"

It was a humongous amount of money. We could buy hamburgers every day, one for each of us — we wouldn't even need to share!

"When can you start?" Mr. Yao asked.

"Tomorrow," my mom and dad blurted out at the exact same time.

Mr. Yao laughed.

As my parents got up to shake his hands, Mr. Yao muttered, "I have to warn you. It's not the nicest motel in the world."

My parents nodded. I could tell it made no difference to them what the motel looked like. It could look like the inside of a Greyhound bus toilet for all we cared; at $150 a day plus free rent, we were in.

CHAPTER 2

The Calivista Motel sat on the corner of Coast Boulevard and Meadow Lane. It was a small motel, the first of three motels in a row. The Topaz Inn and the Lagoon Motel were right next door and bigger, but I immediately decided I liked our little motel the best. With its creamy walls and red doors, it looked warm and inviting. I looked up at the sign and read the words *LOW RATES. CABLE TV. DISNEYLAND — JUST FIVE MILES AWAY.* Excitedly, I asked my parents if that meant we could visit and go on all the rides.

"We probably could!" my mom said.

I smiled, savoring the moment. Our lives were about to change. We were going to become Disneyland-going people.

As if things couldn't get any better, the Calivista had a pool! It was right out in front. The water sparkled under the golden sun. I closed my eyes and pictured myself

16

doing cannonballs in the water all summer long. This was going to be amazing!

Just behind the pool was the front office. I'd asked my parents in the car whether I could help out at the front desk, and my dad had chuckled and said, "We'll see."

Mr. Yao was waiting for us in the front office. He buzzed us in and lifted the divider so we could all get behind the front desk.

The front desk was a long wooden desk that stretched almost the entire width of the room. Just behind the front office were the manager's quarters, where Mr. Yao led us next. There was a living room with a bed in it. He pointed to the bed.

"You guys sleep there," he said to my parents. "So you can hear the customers in the middle of the night."

"Customers come in the middle of the night?" my dad asked.

Mr. Yao nodded. "Of course. It's a motel."

"But won't that wake them up?" I asked.

Mr. Yao rolled his eyes.

"That's the point," he said.

Next he led us over to the small bedroom, just to the right of the living room and the kitchen.

"The girl can sleep here," Mr. Yao said. For some reason, he still kept calling me "the girl" even though I had already told him my name several times.

I put my stuff down in the small bedroom, then joined my parents and Mr. Yao in the front office. Mr. Yao was explaining the buzzer.

"One wrong buzz and it's all over," he said. "See that glass?"

He pointed to the thick glass enclosing the front office.

"That's bulletproof glass. You see a bad guy come up, you don't need to worry. They can't hurt you. But if you press this buzzer . . ."

He put his fingers on the buzzer just under the front desk and a loud *buzz* roared.

"That door right there gets unlocked," Mr. Yao said.

"And then what?" I asked him.

"Then he's inside," Mr. Yao said.

I looked around to see if there were any other magical buttons or bulletproof glass inside the office — there weren't. I asked Mr. Yao how we could tell if someone was a bad guy.

"Based on how they look, of course," he said, which made me wonder, because it's not like bad people walked around with a sticker on their heads saying *I'm bad.*

"The bottom line is, don't let in any bad guys!" Mr. Yao warned. His pupils expanded as he said the word *bad.*

While Mr. Yao took my parents out back to show them the laundry room and cleaning supplies, I stayed in the front office. I climbed up on top of the front desk stool. Gently, I reached down and touched the buzzer with my finger. It was greasy, like it had been pressed hundreds of times. Slowly, I pressed on it and heard it zap. I pressed it again. *Buzz. Buzz. Buzz.* Power coursed through my fingertips.

I closed my eyes and pictured myself checking customers in. *Why, yes, Mrs. Connolly, I'd be glad to show you to your room. Right this way!* I'd say. *Certainly, I can help you with your luggage. It would be my pleasure.*

So deep was I in my fake customer relations that I almost didn't hear it when a real customer walked up and tapped on the front office glass. I looked up to see a thin African American man about fifty or so years old, smiling and waving at me. He motioned with his hand for me to buzz him in.

"Oh, right!" I said, then pressed on the buzzer. *Buzz.*

He pushed open the door and walked in.

"Just saw Mr. Yao in the lot. You must be

the new managers," he said. He extended his hand across the front desk. "Name's Hank."

I smiled, took his hand, and shook it. "I'm Mia. Nice to meet you."

He tilted his head to one side.

"How old are you, Mia?"

"I'm ten," I told him.

"Say, aren't you a little young to be running this place?" he teased me.

I laughed. I liked Hank immediately. "I'm helping my parents," I told him. "What about you? Do you live here?"

"Sure do," he said, and pointed to one of the rooms. "That's me right there. Number twelve."

Hank informed me that he wasn't a regular customer, the kind who stays just a day or two. He was a weekly. A weekly is someone who pays by the week. There were five of them at the Calivista — they were Mrs. Q, Mrs. T, Hank, Billy Bob, and Fred.

"You'll meet them," he said. "They're all nice people."

I smiled.

"Do you guys like living here?" I asked.

"Oh, yeah," he said. "Well, except for Mr. Yao. Everyone hates Mr. Yao."

"Really?" I asked him. "He seems all right."

Intense, but all right.

Hank snorted. "Trust me, he's anything but all right."

Before I could ask Hank what he meant by that, the back door creaked open and my parents and Mr. Yao came back in. When I turned around, Hank was gone.

CHAPTER 3

"Sign here on the dotted line," Mr. Yao said to my parents, presenting them with an enormous employment contract six pages long.

My parents beamed as they proudly signed their names. Mr. Yao took the signed employment contract and stuffed it into his bag.

"Thank you so much, Mr. Yao, for giving us this opportunity," my father said. "You don't know how much it means to us." He got choked up as he said the words.

"We promise we'll take good care of your motel," my mom added. "We won't let you down."

Mr. Yao nodded and held up the manager's keys to the motel. As my parents reached for the keys, he held them just out of reach.

"Everything that happens in this motel is your responsibility, you understand?" he asked. "Something breaks, you have to pay for it."

My parents nodded.

"Under no circumstances are you ever to leave the motel unattended. Ever. One of you must always stay behind."

Again my parents nodded eagerly, even though I was thinking, *Wait — what? I can't go out with both my parents at the same time? But what about Disneyland?*

But it was condition number three that really made my jaw drop.

Mr. Yao turned to me.

"You can't use the pool, kid," he said.

"Why not?" I asked.

"If you use the pool, then all the customers will want to use the pool."

"So?"

"So think of all the water and towels they'll be wasting," he said. "It's not good for the environment."

I frowned at him. Somehow, I doubted this was about the environment.

"She understands. You won't use the pool, will you, Mia?" My mother shook her head at me.

I glanced at my mom, at the desperation in her eyes.

"Okay," I said.

"Good." Mr. Yao grinned, satisfied. He

tossed my parents the keys.

That night, the sweet smells of jasmine tea filled the front office. My parents only ever got the jasmine tea out for special occasions. We had packed a small tin of it before we left China, and every time something good happened, my mom would take out a few leaves and make some tea. I guess not a lot of good things had happened because there was still quite a lot left. But all that was about to change. Tonight, my parents poured generously from the tin.

The calming aroma brought me back to my grandmother's house, all of us crowded around the table. At these big family dinners my cousin Shen and I would always giggle and interrupt each other as we talked.

I felt an ache in my tummy, razor-sharp, at the thought of Shen. I still remembered the day I left. I could see Shen's face pressed up against the glass by the security gate at the airport, blinking furiously, like he was trying hard not to cry. I was too.

On the plane ride over, they gave us little packets of butter for our bread. Butter was very expensive in China, so I asked for extras and put them in my pocket. I saved them for Shen for months in the fridge until it finally sank in that we weren't going back.

So I ate them.

My mother's voice jerked me back to reality.

"Hey, Mia! Look here! Look at me!" she said, smiling.

"Huh?" I asked.

I looked up to see my mother crouching in front of the front desk, holding her hands up like she was going to take a picture. It's this thing she does. My mom says it's important to take pictures of the nice moments in life, even if it's just in your head. As my mom pressed down on her pretend camera, my dad and I sat up straight and gave her our very best smiles.

"Eggplant!" she said in Chinese, and I giggled, because even though that's what people in China said whenever someone took pictures, it was funny hearing it in America.

As my parents unpacked, I slipped out the back to find Hank. I brought him a cup of jasmine tea — now that we were making $150 a day, surely we could afford to buy some more. I had seen a Chinese supermarket on the way over here.

Hank's room was in the back, beside the laundry room. There was a pot of cherry tomato plants in front of his room. I knocked on the door.

Hank answered on the first knock. His eyebrows shot up when he saw the tea.

"That for me?" he exclaimed.

I smiled and handed it to him.

"It's from China," I told him.

"Get out of here!"

The guy next door opened his door to see what was going on. He was a white guy about the same age as Hank. He wore a Hawaiian shirt, and he had a small tattoo of a sailboat on his arm. The smell of popcorn drifted from his room.

"Billy Bob!" Hank said. "Meet Mia. She's the new manager. And look, she brought me some tea from China!"

"Good to meet you, Mia," Billy Bob said, extending a hand.

I shook it.

"Pleasure's all mine," I said.

Billy Bob smiled. "Say, you're a lot nicer than the old manager!"

"The last manager treated us like second-class citizens," Hank added.

"Really?" I asked.

Hank nodded. Carefully, he lifted the cup to his lips and took a sip. "Oh, this stuff is *good.*"

Hank turned to Billy Bob. "You've got to

try this."

More doors opened, and soon all the weeklies were outside, talking and sipping the tea under the glowing crescent. Like Billy Bob, they were white too. Mrs. Q had long wavy hair that ran all the way down her back. Fred had a big belly that shook when he laughed. And Mrs. T had glittery cat-eye reading glasses, which she wore on the tip of her nose. Hank was right — they were all very nice.

The weeklies asked if I wanted to join them for a game of Monopoly, but it was getting late and I needed to help my parents unpack. I bid them all good night and was about to go back to the manager's quarters when I suddenly remembered.

"Hey, Hank, what'd you mean by what you said earlier about Mr. Yao?" I asked. "That he was anything but all right?"

Hank's jaw locked.

"You'll soon find out, kid," Hank said. "The man has coal for a heart."

CHAPTER 4

Hank's words thrashed around inside me. Mr. Yao was strict, sure, maybe even a little dramatic, but coal for a heart? Hank couldn't possibly be right. This was the man who trusted us with his motel, was letting us live here for free, *and* was paying us $150 a day!

The first thing the next day, I intended on setting Hank straight, but when morning came, my mother had other plans.

"Let's go see your new school today!" she announced.

I groaned. Another grade, another year as the new girl. When you've moved as much as I have, checking out schools is like checking out shoe polish. So far, I'd gone to four different schools for five different grades.

Dale Elementary School was about five blocks east from the motel and a lot bigger than my old school. It was late August so classes didn't start for a couple of days. As my mom and I walked across the big empty parking lot, I wondered what kind of kids went there. Nice kids, I hoped. We pushed open the door to the office and the receptionist, a blond lady with big curls that bounced as she moved her head, looked very surprised to see us.

"Can I help you?" she asked.

"Hi. I want to sign my daughter up for school. We just moved here," my mom said.

The receptionist looked me up and down. I wriggled in my tattered pants and big old T-shirt from Goodwill.

"I see," she said. She pushed a button on her desk phone and said, "Principal Evans? We have a new student here to see you."

Principal Evans wore a blazer even though it was ninety degrees outside. She looked like what my mother calls a "powerful white lady." She insisted on taking us on a tour of the school, even though my mom said we didn't need a tour. I could tell she was anxious to get back to the motel.

"It'll only take ten minutes," Principal Evans said, leading us toward the gymnasium in her clickety-clackety black pumps. "So, Mia, tell me about yourself."

I opened my mouth, but before I could say anything, my mom blurted out, "She just moved here from China."

Ugh. Why does she always have to tell people that? It wasn't even true. We'd been here for two years!

Of course, as soon as my mother said the words, Principal Evans started talking to me like I was a turkey.

"Reaaaalllly. Woooow. Hoooowwww doooo youuuu likkke thissss couuuuuntrrrrry?" she asked.

"I really like it," I quickly answered.

Principal Evans put her hand to her chest and exhaled in relief. "You know English! Oh, that's great. I have to admit, we don't get too many Chinese kids here. There's only one other Chinese kid in fifth grade."

She smiled at me and added, "I'm sure he'll be thrilled you're here."

On the way home, my mom and I played our usual game — looking at big American houses and trying to figure out who lived inside.

"A family with two girls," my mom said, pointing to the pink curtains upstairs.

"And a cat," I said. There was a little door in the front door.

I turned to my mom. "Hey, why'd you have to tell the principal I just got here from China?"

"So she'd cut you some slack."

I stopped peering into the houses and peered into my mom. "What do you mean?"

"You heard what she said, there are only two Chinese kids in your grade."

"So?"

"So it probably means most of the other kids are white."

"So?"

"So they'll be way better than you in English," my mom said matter-of-factly.

I looked at the ground.

"Not necessarily," I said. I might not speak native English like Jason, but my English was a lot better than when I first came. I think. Plus, I liked English. I liked how you could say "a train of thought" or "a blanket of snow," which you couldn't in Chinese.

But it didn't matter how much I liked English. My mom had already decided.

"Necessarily," she said.

CHAPTER 5

We were surprised to find the maid cart right where we left it when we got back. It had not moved an inch. In the time that we were gone, my dad had only managed to clean two rooms.

"I don't know how I'm going to get through all these rooms," he said, wiping his sweaty brow with the back of his hand.

"I'll help you," I offered, rolling up my sleeves. In China, I sometimes helped my grandmother scrub her kitchen floor.

"No," my mom said. "I don't want you near that stuff."

She pointed at the maid cart, filled with various colorful bottles of cleaning solutions.

"Then I'll man the front desk!" I said. "I'll call you if I need anything."

I ran out of the room and down the stairs before she could say no.

■ ■ ■ ■

I've got this, I told myself on my way over to the front office. This was not going to be like the restaurant. This time, I was not going to fail. All I had to do was hand out keys and take the cash. How hard could it be?

I got into position, climbing onto the front desk stool and crossing my hands on the desk.

It did not take long before the customers started coming. Unfortunately, when they saw me, the first thing they did was ask to speak to the manager.

So then I had to go get my mom. Up and down the stairs I ran. Every time, she had to stop what she was doing to run down the stairs with me and into the front office, just to hand the customer the key and take the money. By the fifth time, I thought, *Enough.*

I made a little sign and put it on the front desk. It read:

Mia Tang,
Manager

The next time a customer came in and asked to see the manager, I pointed to the sign. And I stared really hard at him.

In science class at my last school, I learned that if you want a mammal to do something, you should stare at it. That's because mammals are social creatures and we're really into hierarchy. At the top, you have your alpha (the leader) and then your betas and omegas. The difference between an alpha and a beta is the alpha wins every staring contest.

So I stared and stared until my eyes went blurry and I was starting to see double and, even then, I refused to blink. Finally, the customer broke down and said, "Okay, okay, fine. I just need a room for the night."

Yes! It worked!

"That'll be twenty dollars, plus tax," I told him.

I watched as he dug into his pocket, pulled out a twenty and a five, and slid the bills across the desk. I gave him back his change and his key. The whole time, I couldn't believe it was really happening. I was just a kid, but I had asked an adult to hand me money and he actually did it!

I repeated my strategy with everyone else who walked through the door that day. Point, stare. Point, stare. Eventually, I didn't even need to stare, people just went ahead and gave me the money. I was so happy, I hopped off the stool, opened up the vending machine, and treated myself to a cream soda.

I got one for Hank too and went to find him. Unfortunately, he wasn't home. Fred, one of the other weeklies, said he was working and wouldn't be home until late.

When I got back to the front desk, the phone was ringing.

The Calivista had an old-fashioned orange phone with a ton more buttons than a usual one. I didn't know what the extra buttons did, and for a second I fantasized that if we pushed the wrong button, the motel would start flying.

"Hello?" I asked, picking up the receiver.

"Is this the front desk?" a voice asked.

I looked at the glowing light and saw that the call was coming from room 6, which I had just rented out to a Mr. Stein.

I cleared my voice.

"Mr. Stein, how can I help you?" I asked, putting on my best customer service voice.

"I need a wake-up call tomorrow at five a.m.," Mr. Stein said.

"Wake-up call. Five a.m.," I repeated. "You got it."

"Don't forget! I have to leave then for a very important meeting!"

I promised I wouldn't and hung up. For the next half hour, I studied the complicated phone system. There was a manual in the drawer, but it was one of those manuals that was impossible to read. It was like the manual they wrote for the walkie-talkies my mom used to make at the factory in China. Her walkie-talkies were great, but when they shipped them to America, nobody could figure out how they worked because the manuals were full of typos and mistakes. I chuckled and wondered if the Calivista phone system was also made in China, like me. It made me feel strangely close to it.

"All right, old friend," I said to the phone system. "Let's do this."

I punched in the code for the wake-up call and entered in the room number and time. To my amazement, the phone system made a beep. It worked!

Pride swelled inside me as I drifted to sleep that night. It was a glorious first day. I'd rented out twelve rooms, seven of which I'd done all by myself. Not only that, I'd gotten the phone system to work. I didn't need to worry about getting up early to wake up Mr. Stein. I could sleep easy, knowing the awesome phone system would do it for me.

Then the morning came.

CHAPTER 6

Mrs. Clifton, from room 5, came running up to the front office at the crack of dawn in her pajamas. She banged on the window.

"Open up! I need to speak to the manager."

My parents and I jumped out of bed and buzzed her in.

"What's wrong?"

"I got a wake-up call for no reason at six a.m., that's why!"

That darn phone system. It must have mixed up waking Mr. Stein in room 6 at 5:00 a.m. with Mrs. Clifton in room 5 at 6:00 a.m.!

At the thought of Mr. Stein, I froze.

I glanced at the clock on the wall. 6:10! He was going to miss his very important meeting!

I raced out the back door in my pajamas and across the motel, nearly crashing into Mr. Stein as his door swung open. Mr. Stein stepped out of his room in his robe, squinting at the morning sun.

"What time is it?" he asked.

I swallowed hard.

We had to give both Mr. Stein and Mrs. Clifton refunds that day. As I handed back the dollar bills I had worked so hard to collect, my dad put his hand on my back while I fought the tears in my eyes. It brought me straight back to Mrs. Fletcher's class last year.

Mrs. Fletcher was my fourth-grade teacher at my last school, and every week, she gave us a spelling quiz. Whoever got all the words right got to hold this special notebook for the day. The cover was rubber, and it looked and smelled like a giant bar of chocolate. You could keep it for a whole day too, which meant anytime you wanted, you could sniff the delicious chocolatey scent. The notebook was filled with little messages and jokes that all the past winners had written down that the rest of us couldn't read. It was like belonging to a special club.

Everyone wanted in on this club, and so did I. But then I started getting my quizzes back and seeing all my mistakes, and the chocolate notebook became as reachable as the moon.

I stopped looking at it, stopped even thinking about it, until one day, toward the end of the year, Mrs. Fletcher called my name.

"The winner today is . . . Mia!" Mrs. Fletcher announced.

The entire class spun around to look at me. They couldn't believe that some kid from China who was still learning English could win, and neither could I. There *had* to be some kind of mistake. But there was no mistaking it — Mrs. Fletcher was walking straight over to me with the notebook. She placed it in my trembling hands, and I held the notebook up to my nose and breathed in deep. As the rich chocolatey smell swirled up my nose, I wanted to cry, I was so happy.

Then I looked up and saw Mrs. Fletcher's face. She was back at her desk, and she was looking over the spelling quizzes again. Something was wrong.

"Wait a minute, hang on. There's a mistake here." She frowned. "Mia, I'm going to need the notebook back."

I shook my head and clutched the notebook tight. *No. You can't do this! You can't take it away — you* just *gave it to me!*

But she did. She got up, walked over, and snatched it from my hands, just as swiftly as

she had placed it there. The velvety chocolate scent, along with the pride in my belly,
disappeared.

That's what giving Mr. Stein and Mrs.
Clifton back their money felt like that day.
As I watched the bills slip away, the money
I had worked so hard for on my first day at
the front desk, I wondered which was better
— to have had something for just a second
and then have it taken away, or to have
never had it at all.

Mr. Yao came by with his son, Jason, later
that day. We weren't expecting him, but
since it was his motel, he could pop in any
time he wanted.

Jason and I sat in the front office while
our parents talked in the living room. While
he fiddled with the keys, I tried to make
conversation.

"So, I checked a bunch of customers in
yesterday," I said.

He barely looked up. He wasn't much of
a talker.

"And it went super well," I said cheerfully.
I left out the part about Mr. Stein and Mrs.
Clifton — he didn't need to know about
that.

In the next room, our parents' voices grew
louder.

"That's *not* what we agreed to," I heard my mom say.

"Says right there in the contract, terms may change from time to time," Mr. Yao replied.

Jason and I looked at each other, and we both ran into the living room.

"But it's only been two days! You said we could have five dollars a customer," my mom said. "Those were your words."

"I said five dollars a customer, not including the first ten and the weeklies."

I jumped to my mother's defense.

"You didn't," I said. "You said five dollars a customer! You never said anything about first ten or weeklies."

"*No!* I heard him say it," Jason insisted.

I narrowed my eyes at him. "You weren't even there! You went to your room," I cut back.

"Enough," Mr. Yao yelled. "That's the deal — take it or leave it."

I looked over at my mom. I could tell she was calculating how much money we'd be losing under the new arrangement. A lot, from the way she was chewing her cheek.

I turned to Mr. Yao and tried again.

"Please," I said to him. "We're working really hard. My parents didn't even finish cleaning until eight last night. And the customers — they aren't so easy to deal with. We had to give two refunds this morning!"

Mr. Yao's eyes bulged. I felt myself shrink from an alpha to an omega.

"You had to give *two* refunds?"

I bit my lip and nodded.

"You're paying for those refunds!" he fumed.

My dad opened his mouth to protest and closed it.

"Go ahead," Mr. Yao said. "Just say the word. There are ten thousand other immigrants who would take your job in two seconds."

The blood drained from my father's face.

"We want the job," he quickly reassured Mr. Yao. "Please, sir. We still really want the job."

The corners of Mr. Yao's mouth turned.

On their way out, Jason leaned over. He had a smug look on his face. "Two refunds, huh? I thought you said it went *super* well yesterday."

I felt my ears boil.

CHAPTER 7

I tried not to think about stupid Mr. Yao and Jason the rest of the day, but it was extremely difficult. How could they just change the terms on us like that? Now whenever a customer returned the key, instead of getting five dollars, we were getting hardly anything.

I counted the keys in my hand. There were eight there. I knew I had checked in twelve people yesterday. The other keys must still be in the rooms.

I hopped off the stool and went out the back to investigate. I found three of the keys in the rooms. The customer just left them there and went on their way, but I could not find the key to room 9. I looked everywhere, but there was absolutely no key in the room. And the customer was long gone.

Did they accidentally take the key?

I walked over to the laundry room, where my parents were washing the towels and sheets. It was this big room way in the back of the motel, which had an industrial washing machine and dryer that ran 24/7 and made this awful grinding noise like it was drying metal screws and not sheets.

Over the noise, I could hear my parents talking.

"Please, sir, we still really want the job?" my mom mimicked my dad. "Why didn't you just kneel before him?"

"Fine, you want to quit? Let's quit!" my dad said. "Let's call him right now and quit!"

"You know we can't quit," my mom said. "Mia's starting school tomorrow!"

At the sound of my name, I thought about turning around and leaving. I hated hearing my parents argue. They hadn't really done it in China, but ever since we came to America, it was getting harder and harder to avoid.

I cleared my throat. "Hey, Mom. Hey, Dad."

"Mia," my dad said, spinning around. He tried to look all happy, like he hadn't just been fighting.

"We were just . . . talking," he said. I wanted to say to them, *It's okay. You argue sometimes. I get it.*

"Room nine left, but he didn't leave his

44

key," I told them. "What should I do?"

"Wait, so there's no key?"

"Well, there's the master key," I reminded them. "But I can't give *that* out."

"All right, let me see what we can do," my mom said.

My mom followed me out of the laundry room. When we got back to the front desk, we opened up all the cabinets. We eventually found a white box buried in the back of a drawer with the words *Official Spare Keys* in permanent marker.

My mom took the box out and opened it. Sure enough, there were thirty official spare keys inside, one for each room.

"Here's the one for room nine," I said, picking it up and clutching it in my hand.

"Great!" my mom said.

I was about to hang the key on its little hook next to all the other keys when it occurred to me. We couldn't give this key out. This was our only spare key. What if someone took it?

My mom sighed. We had no choice but to call Mr. Yao.

As my mom explained the situation to him over the phone, I tried to squeeze in next to her to hear.

"What's he saying?" I asked, but my mom just shook her head.

I went over to my room and picked up the extension just in time to hear Mr. Yao exclaim, "What kind of idiot doesn't charge a deposit on the key?"

That would be me.

For the record, I didn't charge a deposit on the keys because, well, who charges a deposit on keys? Deposits were for renting bikes and cars. Why would anyone want to steal a key?

Mr. Yao told my mom we had to make a new key with the key machine underneath the front desk. My mom and I knelt down to look for it. We finally found it way in the back.

It wasn't actually much of a machine, more like an assortment of blank keys, needles, pins, and files with a big metal thing to keep the key in place as you worked on it.

"Leave it," my mom said. "After I finish cleaning all the rooms, I'll make the key. Until then, don't touch it, okay? Do *not* try to make it." I nodded and waited until she went out the back.

Any adult who says the words *don't touch* to a kid should know it's an open invitation to touch it. I accepted my mom's invitation and picked up one of the blank keys. Holding it up to the spare room 9 key, with all its little ridges and valleys, I wondered: Were we supposed to file the ridges and valleys? Was that how this worked?

I gently ran the file against the blank key. To my surprise, it made a little dent.

I ran the file again. Another dent.

Hey, this wasn't so bad! I didn't even need the metal thing to clamp the key down, I could do it just by holding the key. I filed and filed. With each new dent, I sang, "Look at me! I'm making a key!"

I was having so much fun that I forgot to look at where I was filing and accidentally filed my finger.

"Owwww," I cried.

I dropped the file and the key and held up my throbbing finger. The skin of my index finger had been rubbed raw, and it was bleeding.

I ran to the bathroom to get a Band-Aid, but there weren't any, so I took some toilet paper and wrapped it around my finger. The toilet paper turned bright red in seconds.

I grabbed more toilet paper and held it to the wound even though it hurt like crazy. Eventually the bleeding stopped. I wrapped the toilet paper in Scotch tape, around and around. With my tiny mummy finger all set, I sat back down at the front desk and glanced at the unfinished key.

I should have stopped right there. I should have put the key away and waited for my mom. That would have been the sensible thing to do.

But I had this thing where if I started something, I had to finish it. It didn't matter what it was — books, Chinese chess, or the last strawberry on the candied skewers I used to eat back home. When I started something, I finished it.

And so I picked up the blank key again. With my gigantic finger held high out of the way, I started filing.

Ten minutes later, I was done. It wasn't perfect, I'll admit, and it wasn't pretty by any standard, but when I held the spare to the blank, it had all the same ridges and valleys.

As I stood back to admire my creation, a customer came in.

"Got any rooms in the back?" he asked.

I did indeed and proudly handed him my new key.

"What the hell!" the customer yelled, ringing the office a couple minutes later. "The key you gave me doesn't work!"

As it turned out, though I had filed the

ridges to perfection, I had forgotten to smooth out the edges, so when the customer put the key in, it got stuck. I rushed out the back to help him. We pushed and we pulled. Finally, we managed to jam it into the doorknob and unlock the room.

When the customer laid eyes on the room, his face fell.

"This is a lot smaller than what I was expecting," he said.

I looked around the room. There was a bed, dresser, television, small table, and chair. It was modest, sure. But what else did he need?

"Why don't you get settled in and I'll come back in ten minutes and I'll give you a new key?" I asked.

Mr. Lewis looked like he still wasn't sure about the room and the whole stuck-key thing, so I threw in, "And I'll bring you a free soda — how's that?"

He perked up and said okay.

As I walked back to the front desk, I shook my head. Why was it that everything in America had to do with money? People wouldn't give you back your key unless you charged them a deposit. They'd hold a simple mistake over your head unless you gave them a free soda.

At my old school in China, there was this

kind elderly man who lived near the building. Every day, he'd give me a popsicle on my way home in exchange for telling him what I learned in school that day. That was it. No money. No credit cards. Just "Hey, how was school?"

I sighed. I missed Popsicle Grandpa. There was no one like that here. Here, everything had a price, even kindness.

No sooner had I gotten back to the front office than Mr. Lewis called me back to his room.

"Come back! Come back *right now!*" he said into the phone.

From the urgency in his voice, I thought it was a real emergency. Had the smoke alarm gone off? Did the television explode?

I rushed back to room 9 and found Mr. Lewis standing in the bathroom, staring at the trash can.

"Do you see that?" he asked, pointing at the small plastic trash can under the sink in the bathroom.

I stared into the black bin. I couldn't see anything.

"See what?"

"That!" he shouted. He picked up the trash can and shoved it in my face. I squinted into the darkness and saw what appeared to be a single long string. It looked like dental floss.

"You see it?" Mr. Lewis asked.

"Yes, I see it now," I said.

"This room has *not* been properly cleaned," Mr. Lewis said.

"I assure you, it has —"

"Clearly it hasn't or we wouldn't be having this conversation. I would like another room, a bigger room."

"Sir, all our rooms are the same size."

Mr. Lewis crossed his arms and said, "I don't believe you. I would like you to open up every single room, and I will pick one for myself."

That's when I lost it. Maybe it was my throbbing finger or the two refunds or Mr. Yao changing the deal, but I just couldn't control myself.

"Sir, that's ridiculous! You can't pick your own room. This isn't a salad bar!"

As soon as I said the words, I knew I had gone too far, but it was too late to snatch them back.

"Well!" Mr. Lewis said, fuming. "If that's the way it's going to be, then I would like a refund."

Nooooooo.

"Please, Mr. Lewis," I pleaded with him. "I'm sorry. I shouldn't have said that thing about the salad bar. I don't know why I said that." I squeezed my eyes shut and confessed, "I've never actually been to a salad bar. I've only seen them on TV."

Mr. Lewis looked shocked.

"You've never been to a salad bar?"

I shook my head.

His eyes softened.

"Why are you doing this?" he asked me. "Shouldn't you be out playing?"

I looked away from him. Why were Americans always asking kids to go out and play? In China, kids almost never played. They had to sit for exams starting at an early age. Except for family get-togethers, every minute after school was packed with homework, drilling, revision, and dictation. When I went to first grade in China, I got only two minutes a day to play. That's literally what it said on a schedule I made for myself: *5:00–5:02: Play.*

I wanted to say to Mr. Lewis that I'd never really played and I didn't intend to start now. The other part of me wanted to say, *This* is *playing.* I got to run a motel — was there any better way to play?

In the end, I simply said, "I like my job very much."

Mr. Lewis looked slightly embarrassed and said, "Of course you do. I'm sorry."

He looked around the room once more.

"You know what? This will do just fine," he said.

"Really?" I asked. I could not believe my ears.

"And I'm sorry I gave you such a hard time."

"Here, let me empty that for you," I said, taking the trash can from his hands. I went outside, quickly emptied the can in the Dumpster, and placed it back in Mr. Lewis's bathroom.

"Is there anything I can do to make your stay more pleasant?" I asked him.

Mr. Lewis thought for a second. Then he held up a finger and announced, "Pillows."

"Pillows?"

"Yes, I need four pillows. Two for under my head. One for between my legs, and one to hug."

I smiled.

"Done!"

CHAPTER 8

Who knew that something so basic (pillows) could make someone so happy? After getting Mr. Lewis his pillows and a new key, I went back to the front desk and cut up a bunch of blank cards. I had decided to make customer feedback cards — this way every customer could let us know exactly what they wanted, whether it was extra pillows or extra toilet paper. I put the cards out at the front desk.

The next morning, Mr. Lewis took one of my customer feedback cards and scribbled away. For a long while, I sat and stared at his card, afraid to turn it over — even though he had been nice in the end, I still worried about what it might say. When I finally did turn it over, I braced myself for picky comments regarding the cleanliness of our room or the softness of our pillows.

Never in a million years did I expect to read this message:

There was no greater feeling in the world than reading those words. A smile stretched across my face as I got ready for school.

I decided to wear my blue-and-red shirt and polka-dot leggings on my first day. When I was all set, I said good-bye to my parents and carried my backpack down the four blocks on Meadow Lane. Unlike Coast Boulevard, which was busy and chaotic, Meadow Lane was lined with houses, all with green lawns and mailboxes with little red flags. Still, there were signs that this wasn't completely a "nice" neighborhood, like metal bars on some of the windows and bikes left outside with only the frame left and no wheels.

As I walked, I gave the butterflies in my stomach their usual pep talk — *It's going to be okay. I'll make friends, and if I don't, I'll borrow books from the library.*

This year, there was an additional butterfly. I finally had something cool to tell everyone — I was running a motel! This was sure to blow their minds.

The walls of Dale Elementary School were pink and green. On the pink-and-green walls there hung a big Welcome Back banner, and all around me, kids were scurrying off the bus and into the classrooms. Principal Evans said I was to go to room 12. As I pushed open the pale green door to my new classroom, a roomful of kids turned to look at me.

A tall woman with red hair and big earrings spun around and waved.

"You must be Mia!" the teacher said.

I nodded.

"Welcome! I'm Mrs. Douglas," she said. "Please take a seat!"

I looked around the room. The seats in the back were already taken, and I didn't want to sit in the front. The other kids peered curiously at me. They were mostly white, but there were also a few black kids and Hispanic kids. No Asians.

I took a seat in the middle of the room, next to an empty desk and a poster on the wall that said *Wanted: Children Who Love Reading.*

As more kids piled in, Mrs. Douglas asked us to go around the room and tell everyone something about ourselves.

"Doesn't have to be big," she said. "Just has to be something . . . *interesting.*"

"Can it be weird?" someone asked.

Mrs. Douglas's eyes opened wide.

"I *love* weird!" she exclaimed.

We went in alphabetical order, so Allen

56

Adelman had to go first. I watched as he agonized over something sufficiently weird.

He finally went with "I collect things."

"What kind of things?" the other kids asked.

"Rocks, key chains," he said.

My new classmates yawned. *Not weird.*

"Bottle caps, postcards too."

Still not weird.

"And fingernails!" Allen quickly added. "All my old clippings!"

Whoops, too weird. Allen immediately put his hand over his mouth, but it was too late. The other kids stared at him like he was a crow. Allen shriveled under their gaze.

Next came Bethany Brett, who looked like she had about fifteen something specials about her and couldn't *wait* to get started. She told us all about her golf game and how she went to this fancy ice-skating camp this summer. "Now I can do jumps and twirls and everything!" she bragged. Mrs. Douglas beamed at her, clapping her hands wildly, and we all knew who was going to be teacher's pet this year.

When it was my turn, I took a deep breath. *Here goes!*

"Hi, I'm Mia. I live and work in a —"

I was just about to say "motel" when the door swung open.

"Sorry I'm late!" a voice boomed.

I turned around and, walking through the door with his shirt half tucked in his pants, looking like he just woke up, was Jason Yao.

"So, Mia, what were you going to say?" Mrs. Douglas asked.

"Nothing," I muttered.

I couldn't believe it. What were the chances of Jason being in the same school, let alone the same class as me? Not only was Jason here, but because he was late, he had to take the only empty desk left, which was right next to mine. Great.

"You were about to tell us something. You live and work in a — ?"

Jason shot me a look. A *don't you dare* look. Heat rushed to my cheeks and to Jason's. *Why didn't he want the others to know?*

"Nothing. Just a normal house," I quickly lied. "With a dog."

"What kind of dog?" the other kids were curious.

"A golden retriever." It was the only type of dog I knew.

"What color?"

"Uhhh . . . golden?" I tried.

The other kids nodded, satisfied with this information. I let out a sigh of relief as Mrs. Douglas moved on to the next person, while my least favorite person in the world sat in his seat glaring at me.

Jason marched up to me at recess.

"Let's make one thing clear," Jason said. "You don't know me and I don't know you. Got it?"

"Whatever," I said.

Jason turned and walked away.

"What was that all about? Was he bothering you?" someone asked. It was a girl from my class who had walked over. Guadalupe Garcia, I think her name was, or Lupe for short.

"No," I quickly said. Lupe looked like she didn't believe me.

"A little," I admitted.

"Jason can be *so* annoying," she said, shaking her head. I smiled.

"Hey, what happened to your finger?" Lupe asked, pointing. I'd taken the toilet paper off and replaced it with a proper Band-Aid my mom gave me (along with an earful on how I should have waited for her).

"Nothing," I said, hiding the wound with my thumb.

"So you have a golden retriever?" Lupe asked.

I nodded slowly. Lupe smiled.

"Me too."

Lupe went on to tell me that on top of a golden retriever, she had two other dogs, a pug and a Shiba Inu.

"Shibas are the hardest to train, because they're so smart," she informed me. I nodded politely and concurred that training was very important.

She asked me what my dog's name was, and I blurted out Sonjay, because I was still thinking about Jason, and Sonjay was Jason flipped around. It just came out.

"Sonjay, really," Lupe said. "That's an unusual name."

I quickly tried to change the subject. "So what'd you do this summer?" I asked.

Lupe told me all about her awesome summer and how her parents bought her this giant trampoline. It was in her backyard, and she recently did a flip but her dad wasn't there to see it because he had to go on a business trip.

I couldn't stop staring at her, this girl with a house, a trampoline, and three dogs. She sounded so *normal.*

She asked me if I had a trampoline.

"No . . ." I said. Then my face brightened. "But I have a pool!"

"A pool?" she gasped, her eyes opening wide. "That's amazing!"

"It is pretty amazing," I told her.

I didn't tell her the part about how I wasn't allowed to go in. Just look at it.

Toward the end of recess, I left Lupe to go check out the library. She wanted to come with me, but I told her I'd only be five minutes. I didn't want her to know what I wanted to look up, which was the price of an electronic key machine. My finger was still throbbing and I wondered how much a safer (and easier) machine would cost.

As I walked toward the library, I heard voices down a dark, empty corridor. It sounded like some kids fighting. I tiptoed closer to get a better look. From the shadows, I could make out four big kids — they looked like sixth graders — and they were huddled around another kid.

My breath stopped short when I saw who the kid in the middle was. It was Jason.

"Take that, Chinese dough boy!" the sixth graders taunted him. One of them had his hand on Jason's arm and was twisting it while the other boys were holding Jason back.

"Oowwww," Jason cried.

"That's what you get for being a know-it-all," the sixth graders said. Jason howled as they twisted his arm even harder.

"Stop!" I yelled.

The boys spun around and froze. One of the sixth graders smirked.

"Look, Chinese dough boy has a girlfriend!" he exclaimed. My cheeks turned bright red.

"I'm not his girlfriend!" I shot back. "I'm not even his friend."

Just then, a teacher started walking over.

"Hey, what's going on?" he hollered.

"Shoot!" the sixth graders yelled. Quickly, they let go of Jason and scrambled out of there.

After the sixth graders ran away, Jason and I walked silently back to class. I kept looking over at the bruise developing on his arm. I wanted to ask him if he was okay, but then I thought about all the horrible things he and his dad said the day before, and I didn't.

CHAPTER 9

I walked home by myself after school, looking over my shoulder as I made the crossing
from Meadow Lane onto Coast Boulevard.
It was like crossing over into a different
world. Back at the motel, I dashed to find
my parents to tell them the news that Jason
Yao was in my class, but as it turned out,
they had other problems to worry about.

The washing machine in the laundry room
was busted. There was water everywhere
and my dad had foam up to his knees.

"Quick," he said, pointing to a bucket.
"Hand me that."

I gave him the bucket. It filled in a matter
of seconds and I dragged it out of the
laundry room to the parking lot, watching
as the murky water spilled onto the ground
like a tidal wave. As soon as it emptied, I
took it back into the laundry room. Fill and
spill. Fill and spill.

When the last of the water was emptied

and the laundry room all wiped down, my parents got on the phone with Mr. Yao. I picked up the receiver in my room so I could listen in.

"What now?" Mr. Yao barked.

"I'm terribly sorry, but we're going to need a new washing machine," my dad said.

"What did you do? Did you break it?" Mr. Yao asked, annoyed. "You idiot!"

"He's not an idiot!" I yelled into the phone.

"Mia, get off the phone," my dad said.

I said okay and put the phone down on the table for a second, then very quietly picked it back up.

"You're paying for it. And guess what? They're not cheap," Mr. Yao said.

"Mr. Yao, please, be reasonable," my dad pleaded. "I didn't break it. I just got here. I've barely even touched it!"

"Well, you must have done something, because now it's broken. And if you want a new washing machine, you're going to have to pay for it," Mr. Yao said before slamming down the phone.

My mother was so furious after the call, she was shaking.

"That man," she shrieked. But no matter how mad she got, there was no avoiding the fact that we had to get a new washer. Mr.

Yao had told my dad right before he got off the phone that it would take several days before it could be delivered.

My dad paced back and forth in the living room, trying to figure out how we were supposed to live without a washing machine for so long. Every day, the tower of dirty towels from the customers was as tall as me.

"Maybe we could send it out," my dad said, thinking out loud, then quickly shook his head when he thought about how much that would cost. And who would be paying for it? Certainly not Mr. Tightwad.

"What if we told people not to use so many towels?" I suggested.

Again, my dad shook his head.

"We're a motel. We have to have towels," he said. With a sigh, he turned to my mom and said, "We're just going to have to wash them all by hand."

My mom groaned. On top of all the other things they had to clean.

It didn't take long before the laundry room was teeming with towels. There were piles and piles of them, sitting in buckets, on the floor, hanging on the door. Every time I walked by the laundry room, there seemed to be more of them — like the towels were meeting each other in the laundry room, getting married, and having babies.

I knew I had to do something, so I went around to all the weeklies and explained the situation. They were all very sympathetic. They vowed to limit their towel usage to one towel a day until the new washer arrived.

"Thanks so much for understanding," I said to Hank. He and Billy Bob were in Hank's room cooking hamburgers on Hank's hot plate.

"Not a problem," Hank said, throwing patties onto the pan. They didn't have enough ground beef, so Hank was taking a bunch of saltines and mushing them up. Then he added the ground-up cracker crumbs to his ground beef.

I watched as he shaped the crumbly ground beef mixture expertly into more patties.

"Wow, it looks just like a real hamburger," I said to Hank.

"Oh, sure, it tastes like one too," he said, handing me a cooked one.

Gingerly, I lifted the saltine burger to my mouth and took a bite. He was right! It tasted just like the real thing, only crunchier. I devoured the burger.

"I'm sorry you guys have to pay for the new washer," Hank said as he threw more patties onto the sizzling pan. "Typical Mr. Yao. Squeezing us for every last penny!"

He handed me another saltine burger. As I chewed, I thought about how nice it was that Hank lumped us together with the weeklies rather than Mr. Yao.

Despite all our efforts, the mountain of towels continued to grow at an alarming rate. There just wasn't enough time to wash all of them by hand every night. That Sunday, I promised to help my dad knock out a bunch of them.

We put them into buckets, filling the buckets with water and dumping in the laundry detergent. Then we sat down and scrubbed them by hand until our fingers turned into raisins. Even then, there were still dozens of dirty towels left — so many, in fact, that we soon ran out of buckets.

"We're going to have to go over to the Home Depot and buy more buckets," my dad said, shaking his head.

Buckets were $4.99 each. That was more than a Big Mac cost, and we couldn't even afford those. But I had an idea. I grabbed as many of the rest of the dirty towels as I could and ran toward one of the empty guest rooms.

"Follow me," I said to my dad.

I headed straight for the bathroom, where I dumped the dirty towels in the bathtub, ran the water, and sprinkled the laundry detergent.

"But how are we going to scrub them?" my dad asked.

I grinned at him and started rolling up my pants. As soon as my dad saw that, he smiled and started rolling his up too. We jumped into the tub together, the water sloshing and splashing as the wet towels tickled our toes. We made so much noise jumping and screaming and laughing that my mom came to see what was going on.

"What are you guys doing?" she asked.

We froze when we saw her, bracing for a lecture, but when I peeked at her face, I didn't find a frown.

"Scoot over," she said.

My mom started rolling up her pants. That afternoon, my parents and I hopped and hopped and hopped, laughing so hard, we soon forgot we were washing towels.

CHAPTER 10

Two days later, the new washing machine arrived while my dad and I were working, as did an unexpected guest: Uncle Ming. Uncle Ming wasn't really my uncle — that was just what we called family friends in China. But he had worked in the same hot, sweaty kitchen as my dad last year, and we hadn't seen him since then.

How he managed to drive himself to the Calivista, I had no idea, because smoke was coming out from the hood of his car when he arrived, *and* the bumper was falling off. And Uncle Ming himself actually looked *worse* than his car. He had a swollen black eye and bruises all over his cheeks and neck.

"What happened to you?" my dad asked, rushing over to help his wounded friend inside. He led Uncle Ming into the kitchen. Uncle Ming winced as he slid into the chair, like it hurt even to sit.

"It's a long story," he said. His thick

Beijing accent made me feel like I was back home. He lifted his puffy eyes and peered at my dad. "It's good to see you, old friend."

My dad gave Uncle Ming a hug while I took out his things and put them inside one of the guest rooms — room 1, the nicest one.

When I got back, the two were deep in conversation, talking about sharks, of all things. That was weird. I didn't want to disturb them, so I stood in the corridor listening.

"But why, Ming, why did you go to the loan sharks?" my dad asked.

"I wasn't planning on it. But then I lost my job. . . ." Uncle Ming said. "And a hundred dollars turned into five hundred dollars . . . and before I knew it . . ."

"How much do you owe them?"

"Five thousand dollars," Uncle Ming said. His voice cracked as he said the number.

My dad said a swear word in Chinese.

"What do I do, buddy? They're going to kill me if I don't pay up . . ." Uncle Ming cried.

I gasped at the word *kill*. They both looked up at me and immediately dropped the subject. They didn't bring up sharks or loans again the whole evening. That didn't stop me from thinking about it, though.

■ ■ ▪ ■

After dinner, while my parents and Uncle Ming reminisced about China, I slipped out the back door. Hank wasn't in his room, but Billy Bob's lights were on. I peered inside and saw that the weeklies were just starting another game of Monopoly.

"Mia!" they exclaimed when Billy Bob opened his door. "Come and join us!"

I grinned. I loved Monopoly.

"Can I be the hat?" I asked them, plopping down on Billy Bob's bed. The hat in Monopoly looked nice. It looked like a rich man's hat. The shoe, on the other hand, looked like a poor man's shoe.

"You can be anything you want," Billy Bob said, handing me the hat. He selected the racecar for himself and the iron for Hank. Fred picked the wheelbarrow.

Quickly, we set up the game. Billy Bob and Fred made me the bank. As we played, I turned to Hank and asked him if he knew anything about loan sharks.

"Oh, that's nothing you want to get involved with," he said. "No, sirree. You want to stay as far away as you can from that rabbit hole!"

He explained that a loan shark was some-

71

one who loaned people money with very high interest.

"What's interest?" I asked him.

"Interest is like a fee you pay the person for borrowing the money. So if you want to borrow ten dollars from me, I would say okay, but you gotta give me twelve dollars back. Otherwise, what do I get out of it? So that two dollars is interest," he said.

"But a loan shark," Billy Bob jumped in. "A loan shark doesn't want twelve dollars back. He wants twenty dollars back or even fifty dollars."

"Fifty dollars?" I asked. "What kind of people would agree to that?"

"Desperate people," Hank said. "People who can't get loans anywhere else."

"And what happens if they don't pay them back?"

Hank sucked in air. "You don't want to know," he said.

I turned to Fred.

"They'll come and find you," Fred said. "Beat you up . . . or worse."

I felt myself go cold. Just then, Hank let out a squeal.

"Hot diggity dog! Will you look at that? I now own Pennsylvania Avenue *and* Park Place!" Hank howled with glee. "Pay up, Mia, that'll be fifty dollars a night."

I handed him fifty dollars. Hank took the Monopoly money and kissed it.

"Someday, Mia," he said softly. "Someday . . ."

"Someday what?" Billy Bob asked, chuckling. "You'll *really* own Pennsylvania Avenue and Park Place?"

"Hey, it can happen! If it can happen in Monopoly, why not in real life?" Hank insisted. "Isn't that right, Mia?"

I looked at Hank. I had a feeling he was just trying to make me feel good, but I thought I saw a glimmer of hope in his eyes too.

"Right!" I quickly said.

CHAPTER 11

Uncle Ming stayed for three days, until he could get his car fixed. With his broken English, he had a hard time communicating with garages, so I helped him call one up that was close by. At first, they weren't so keen to help.

When they heard my voice, they said, "Sorry. We don't work on toy cars."

I called back, and this time, I borrowed a line from my customers.

"I'd like to speak to the manager," I said.

In the end, I got the manager to send someone over to the motel to take a look at Uncle Ming's car. The repair guy told Uncle Ming he had a radiator problem. They managed to drive the car over to the garage, where they fixed it for him, but when it came time to settle the bill Uncle Ming came horribly short. We'd given him fifty dollars, which was just about all the extra cash we had, what with Mr. Yao changing the deal and making us pay for the washing machine. But the total bill was $200.

So then Uncle Ming tried something crazy. He tried to pay the rest in coupons. He'd been collecting coupons from all over — there were coupons for free chicken nuggets at McDonald's, free haircuts at Supercuts, and free frozen yogurt. There were even coupons for free foot massages.

"You can't pay in coupons!" the garage manager wailed. "What am I going to do with free foot massages?"

"We'll take them!" his mechanics blurted out from the back of the garage.

"Please, sir," Uncle Ming begged the manager. "It's all I have."

The manager looked at Uncle Ming for a while, and after much deliberation, he sighed. He took the fifty dollars and the coupons, which he distributed to his mechanics. Everybody cheered. I couldn't believe it!

We all waved as Uncle Ming drove away. He promised to return soon and to pay my parents back the fifty dollars. My dad told him not to worry about it and to focus on getting far, far away from the loan sharks.

In school that week, Mrs. Douglas asked us to write a short story. I *really* wanted to write about the loan sharks, but I didn't know if that was too out there, so I tried to look around to see what other people were writing. Next to me, Jason was scribbling furiously, covering his words with his hand as he wrote. I leaned over, trying to peek at his writing, but Jason shifted his body, blocking my view with his arm. *Great,* now he had an arm wall.

He turned to me and hissed, "Stop it!", then narrowed his eyes at me.

"Mia, eyes on your own paper please." Mrs. Douglas frowned.

She said it like I was cheating. I opened my mouth in protest, then closed it. I blew at my bangs in frustration instead and plunged my eyes down on the blank page in front of me.

"Remember, show, not tell! Write what you feel, kids," Mrs. Douglas announced to the class. "If you're mad, write mad. If you're sad or you're worried, write sad and worried."

I was all those things. I thought about Uncle Ming and his black eye and the way his voice rose and fell like a curtain when he said, *What do I do, buddy? They're going to kill me. . . .*

But when I put my pencil down onto the paper, do you know what marched onto the page? Puppies and houses.

■ ■ ■ ■

At lunch, Lupe sat next to me picking at her turkey sandwich while I gobbled up my free school spaghetti.

"Why were you looking at Jason's paper?" Lupe asked. "You don't like him, do you?"

"Are you kidding? I can't stand him!"

"Good, because he's terrible," Lupe said.

"You don't even know the half of it," I muttered, shaking my head. "So what'd you write about?"

"I wrote about how last weekend my parents and I waited in line at the movies for an *hour,* and when we finally got up to the ticket booth lady, they were sold out! Isn't that sad?"

"That is super sad," I said, wishing, hoping, one day that would be my super sad.

"What about you? What'd you do this weekend?" she asked.

I turned to tell her about Uncle Ming, then thought *nah.* She wouldn't get it. That was so beyond the world of movies and trampolines and Shiba Inus.

"Just played with my dog," I lied.

After lunch, we went to PE. We were playing softball that day. Both Lupe and I stood way out in left field, as far away from the action as we could, since we both hated sports.

Actually, I didn't really *hate* sports. We just didn't have any medical insurance, and my parents didn't want me "taking any chances."

"What if you break your arm?" my mom asked when I started going to school in America. "What if a ball comes flying, hits you in the head, and you have to have stitches?"

Back in China, this would have been no problem, as my uncle was a doctor. Whenever I got sick, he'd come over and take care of me. My uncle always wore his stethoscope around his neck, and when we left for America, he gave it to my dad to take with him.

"I wish I could take *you* with me," my dad said to his brother.

"I'm sure there are doctors in America," my uncle said with a chuckle.

It turned out, there were doctors. Just not for us.

So my mom made me promise every morning that I'd stay on the sidelines during gym class. It wasn't always easy to just stand and watch, but now at least I had Lupe with me.

Today, we were so busy chatting we didn't even notice when the softball landed right next to us. Lupe glanced at the ball and went right back to chatting. She didn't even pick it up.

She must *really* hate sports.

Chapter 12

Instead of going straight home after school that day, I took the long way back, stopping at various restaurants. I was collecting brochures for the front office. Mr. Yao may be an unbelievable cheapskate, but there were some free things we could do to spruce up the place, like putting flyers out for local establishments. Or collecting customers' mailing addresses, which I'd already started doing. Anytime a customer checked in, I asked them for their home address so if they left something behind, I could mail it back to them.

I was in the middle of sorting through the mountain of brochures and menus when a slightly disheveled-looking white man walked up and tapped on the glass.

He was tapping furiously, like it was an emergency, so I buzzed him in. That was when it hit me — the sour stench of sweat and alcohol. My throat tightened as the wave of stink crashed into the room. The man was completely drunk. I should *not* have buzzed him in.

"I neeeda rooooom," he slurred, stumbling toward me. He steadied himself by holding on to the front desk with both hands. "Gimmme a room!"

"Uhhh . . . I need to go get my parents. Wait right here," I told him, desperate to get away from this guy.

As I hopped off the stool, I realized, *Wait a minute, I can't leave him here.* He could reach over and take all our cash from the cash drawer. He had to go back out!

"Actually, can you wait outside?" I asked timidly.

He did not like the sound of that. The man turned to me with his bloodshot eyes and pounded his hand on the counter.

"What did you say?" he bellowed.

My mind was racing. I could probably still get out of there if I let him stay inside. But then what about the cash?

"Please, sir," I tried again. "I just need you to wait outside."

"Why? Why can't I stay right here?" he demanded.

"You just can't!" I shouted. I glanced out the window, searching for my parents, but they were still upstairs cleaning.

Suddenly, he grabbed me by my shirt. "Are you jerking me around, kid? Are you?"

"No, sir." I shook my head from side to side. His rancid breath stung my eyes. With my fingers, I tried to reach for the phone, but his grip on my shirt was too tight.

"Please just calm down," I pleaded with him. I thought maybe I could distract him with all my restaurant brochures. "Hey, are you hungry? I have a bunch of menus —"

"I don't want to see some damn menu," he screamed into my face. "I want a motel room!"

The next thing I knew, he pounded the counter so hard, the wood nearly chipped. I screamed. Tears streamed down my eyes. Through the blur of my tears, I saw a figure outside, banging on the front office door.

It was Hank!

Quickly, I reached down and pressed on the buzzer. Hank stormed inside.

"What the hell do you think you're doing?" Hank hollered at the drunk man. "Let her go!"

The drunk man instantly dropped his hands, and I gasped for air, like I'd been holding my breath the entire time.

Hank raised his fists. "Get out of here before I call the cops!" he yelled.

The drunk man dragged himself out of

the front office, muttering under his breath, "She was jerking me around, man."

When he finally disappeared around the corner, Hank turned to me.

"You all right?" he asked.

I shook my head. I lifted the divider and collapsed into his arms. I clung to him and cried, shaking with fear, blind with gratitude. What would have happened to me had Hank not come in? The thought crushed the breath out of me.

"Shhh. It's okay," Hank comforted me, patting my arm.

But it wasn't okay. I thought I could make the front desk better with all my spare keys and comments cards. But no card in the world could protect me from what I'd been avoiding since day one: One wrong buzz and it was all over.

This was not just fun and games.

This was dangerous.

CHAPTER 13

I didn't wash my shirt after the drunk guy left. Instead, I draped it over a chair in my room. It was a reminder of what could happen any day. And every morning, when I opened my eyes, I would look at it, at the spot where he had grabbed me, and wonder how we could make the Calivista safer.

I came up with three possible ways.

1. Install bulletproof glass up and down the front desk. That way, even if I buzzed in the wrong person, there was still an additional layer of protection between me and the customer.
2. Install a security camera in the front office. It would be doubly great if the video feed went directly to a certain channel on all the motel TVs. That way my parents could see what was going on in the front of-

fice while they were cleaning each
room and come down if I needed
help.
3. Install a panic button right under
   the front desk to call the police. It
   would work just like a buzzer. All
   I'd have to do was press it and the
   police would come.

Later that week, I told Mr. Yao my ideas
when he came by. He immediately shot
them down.

"All that stuff costs money. You think
money grows on trees?"

"I checked at the library and bulletproof
glass only costs twenty-five dollars," I told
him.

I glanced at Jason, who, as usual, came
with his dad and, as usual, didn't say
anything helpful.

"Twenty-five dollars *per square foot.* And
that doesn't include the installation," Mr.
Yao said.

"What about the security camera?" I
asked. "That can't be that expensive. You
could put it —"

"No," Mr. Yao interrupted.

"Please, just hear me out . . ." I said.

"The answer is *no,*" Mr. Yao snapped.

I looked over at my mom and my dad, but

they just shook their heads. *Let it go,* my dad mouthed. He had dark circles under his eyes from checking customers in all last night.

"Why don't we go outside?" my parents suggested to Mr. Yao. "Let us show you the new washing machine."

Mr. Yao nodded and followed my parents out the back.

Jason stayed behind, fiddling with the restaurant menus. Quietly, he muttered, "I think the security camera is a good idea."

I almost didn't hear him.

"What?" I asked.

"The security camera," he said. "It's not a bad idea."

I stared at him.

"Well, why didn't you say so?" I asked him. He shrugged.

I know why — because he was too chicken to stand up to his dad. I shook my head at him. Coward.

Mr. Yao came back and told Jason it was time to go. Jason hopped off the stool, took a few menus from my collection, and stuffed them into his pocket. I followed them out to the parking lot.

"Mr. Yao," I tried one last time. "If you'll just go home and think about what I said . . . It really wouldn't cost much and it would make the motel so much safer."

Mr. Yao stopped walking and turned to me.

"You know what's the difference between a good employee and a bad employee?" he asked, jabbing his finger into my chest at the exact spot the drunk guy grabbed me.

I shook my head.

"It's not whether they're hardworking or even whether they're smart," he said, staring into my eyes. "It's whether they know their place."

As he and Jason piled into their car and drove away, I stood in the parking lot for a long, long time. The hot California sun blazed down on me, yet I felt no warmth.

CHAPTER 14

"What's wrong?" Lupe asked me at recess the next day.

All day, I'd been walking around with a humongous cloud over my head. The sadness must have been leaking out of my eyes because Lupe kept looking at me. And of course the more she looked at me, the more I wanted to tell her.

But how? How would I say to her a drunk guy grabbed me, clutched a fistful of my shirt, and screamed into my face? That the man I was working for didn't think my life was worth twenty-five dollars per square foot?

How could I tell Lupe all that?

"Oh, c'mon, it can't be that bad," she said, which didn't make it feel better at all.

It only made me mad because, really, she had no idea what she was talking about. As much as I liked Lupe, she was just in a different world. Her and her perfect parents and her perfect dogs. It just wasn't fair!

I stood up. "I'm sorry, I just need to be alone right now," I told her, and walked away.

I wandered down the hallway and ended up in the empty auditorium. There was a piano in the front, so I went and sat down on its bench. Back in China, I used to play a little with my cousins, because a friend of my aunt was a teacher and gave us free lessons on Sundays. I had learned Beethoven, Bach, and some simple Mozart. Of course, I hadn't touched a piano since I came over here.

Gently, I lifted the cover. To my surprise, it wasn't locked. With a trembling finger, I pressed down on the middle C.

I closed my eyes, feeling the note. *Oh, C, how I've missed you.* I picked up my other hand and ran my fingers up and down the familiar black and white keys. Slowly, I began playing "Für Elise." I thought I might have forgotten it — it had been two long years — but I still remembered it!

The notes carried me far, far away. I felt weightless, soaring across an ocean of memories. I thought of my cousin Shen, how the two of us used to get all dressed up for piano recitals, me in my silk *qipao* and him in his embroidered *changshan.* We'd point at each other in our old-fashioned Chinese outfits and giggle, even though deep down inside, we were both so proud to be wearing them. Then, as the curtain rose, we'd mouth, *You can do it,* to each other, a flurry of excitement as we stepped onto the stage. Closing my eyes, I could almost see Shen. My fingertips could almost touch him!

When I got to the dramatic section, fear poked in. This was the part I used to always mess up on.

"Why put a scary part in the middle of a beautiful piece?" I remember asking my piano teacher.

"Because life is scary sometimes, little one," he had said.

I was only five at the time and didn't quite understand. Now, when I played the dramatic section, my chin quivered. I felt a sob building within me as I thought about Mr. Yao and how he just took and took and took. How he refused to spend twenty-five dollars a square foot to protect us even though twenty-five dollars was *nothing* to him; it was probably what he paid for dinner. I thought about my father, robbed of sleep, jolted awake by customers, night after night. And my mother, the way her eyes twitched at the supermarket checkout counter every time the cashier scanned a new item and the total price jumped. I thought about Hank and his saltine burgers, and Uncle Ming and the loan sharks, and before I knew it, tears were streaming down my cheeks. As my feelings coursed through my fingers into the sad music, I suddenly heard a sound from the back. Someone was in the auditorium listening to me.

I instantly stopped playing and jumped up from the piano. I hugged myself with my arms, like I was naked.

"Hello?" I called.

The small figure made its way over to me. When I saw who it was, my stomach lurched.

"What are you doing here?" I asked Jason.

Jason ignored my question and asked, "Where'd you learn to play like that?"

"I had a teacher in China," I said. "What do you care?"

"You learned to play like that in China?" he repeated. There was a flash of surprise in his eyes.

I nodded.

"But my father said there's nothing in China except piles of dirt and trash," he said.

"Your father's a *liar*," I said angrily. A typhoon ripped through me. My hands balled into fists, prepping for battle.

"He said that you guys liked to sit around and spit on the floor."

"That's absurd!" I exclaimed.

"Is it true none of you had any money?" he asked.

That part was, unfortunately, true. My parents came to America with only $200 in their pocket.

"How'd you learn to play piano if you had no money?" Jason asked.

For some reason, this infuriated me.

"Why can't I learn piano?" I asked him. "What, you think only rich people get to do stuff?"

Jason's face turned bright red. "I just meant —"

"Poor people can do stuff too!" I shouted at him as I slammed the piano cover and walked away.

CHAPTER 15

"Honey, we've been thinking," my dad said when I got home from school that day. I was still mad about my conversation with Jason. "Maybe it's not such a good idea you watch the front desk."

"Clearly, it's dangerous," my mom said. "After what happened —"

"No," I said firmly. *That* was not the solution. "And besides, who's going to watch it if I don't?"

"I will," my mother said.

I shook my head. "Dad can't clean all the rooms by himself." He was barely managing as it was, even with my mom, and they still wouldn't let me anywhere near the maid cart because of the chemicals. Every day, the two of them cleaned until well past sunset. They had both lost so much weight. They constantly had sweat stains on their shirts and smelled of Clorox.

"I can manage by myself," my dad insisted.

"No you can't." I turned to my mom. "Sorry, Mom. I'm not giving you my job." The front desk was my chocolate notebook and I was not letting it go. No way.

I plopped down on the front desk stool and gazed at the wallpaper, at the spot where the security camera was supposed to go.

"Why can't we just tell him he *has to* get us some cameras? Or else?" I asked my parents.

"Because he knows there's no 'or else,' " my dad said softly.

I bit my lip.

"It's just so unfair," I said.

My mother sighed. She walked over and put a hand on my shoulder.

"We're immigrants," she said. "Our lives are never fair."

My dad nodded. "We have to try," he said. "We have to try and accept our fate."

My parents were always going on about fate. Sometimes I wondered if this fate thing was just something adults made up to make themselves feel better, like the tooth fairy.

"And really, it's not so bad," my dad said, his face brightening. "We have a roof over our heads. We have each other."

"That's right," my mom said.

"It could be a lot worse. Look at Ming," my dad added. He didn't mention the loan sharks, but he didn't need to. We were all thinking it.

My parents let me keep my job, but only after I told them I would make a sign saying *Security Camera Installed* and put it up in the front office. Even though we didn't have a security camera, people could *think* we had a camera.

Billy Bob, one of the weeklies, came into the front office. He pointed at the sign and asked, "Where's the new security camera?"

I looked down at my hands.

"There isn't one," I admitted.

I told him about Mr. Yao and how he rejected all my ideas because they were too expensive.

Billy Bob sighed.

"I'm sorry to hear that," he said. "But you know what? Come here, let me show you something."

I followed him out to the parking lot. The two of us stood in front of Billy Bob's old blue station wagon.

"See that sticker on my car?" Billy Bob asked, pointing to a shiny sticker on the driver's side window.

I squinted at the words. It said *Don't Touch! Alarm System Installed.*

Billy Bob leaned over, cupped his hand, and whispered into my ear, "There's no alarm system."

I smiled.

Later that day, a small hatchback pulled up beside Billy Bob's station wagon. A Chinese guy came bouncing out of it, running up to my dad and shaking his hand furiously. He told him he was a friend of Uncle Ming's and asked if he could stay here for the night.

"Any friend of Ming's is a friend of mine." My dad smiled.

That night, as my mom prepared dinner, Uncle Li stood next to her, beaming at the sweet and sour pork, rubbing his hands while the wok sizzled.

"I haven't even tasted it, and I *know* it's delicious," he praised my mother, who blushed with pride.

"Thanks," my mom said.

"You don't know what it's been like for me these last few months," Uncle Li said.

He told us that he met Ming working in the kitchen of a burger place.

"All day, we'd make these juicy burgers for the customers, you know the kind with real thick beef?"

My stomach nodded.

"That's why I took the job — for the burgers! But for lunch, you know what the boss would give us? A sandwich of two slices of white bread and some mayonnaise. The whole thing was white!"

"No meat?" my dad asked.

"No meat."

"No lettuce?" my mom asked, popping a spring roll into her mouth as she sat down.

"How about some tomato?" I asked.

"Nope. Just white on white on white, day after day after day."

White on white on white? That's not a sandwich — that's an envelope!

My father shook his head at his new friend's misfortune.

"So you know what I did?" the man asked, leaning in, as if to let us in on a secret.

"What?"

"Every day I made a delicious hamburger and wrapped it up carefully. I put it in a bag, and then I threw it into the trash," he said. "Then, every day after work, I'd go find it."

"You WHAT?" My mother dropped her chopsticks.

Everyone stopped eating.

"It wasn't always easy, let me tell you. Some days, my body was completely inside

97

the Dumpster and all you'd see were these two little legs kicking in the air. But I *always* managed to find my burger in the end," he said triumphantly.

My eyes slid over to the trash can in the kitchen, overflowing with potato peels and eggshells. I pictured two little legs sticking out.

"Did anyone ever see you?" I asked.

He shrugged, like *So what if they did?* I marveled at the guy, at his bravery. He didn't even care if anyone saw him — that was the amazing part. I think I definitely would have cared.

"When I found my burger, it was the most incredible feeling ever. I devoured it right then and there, I couldn't wait," he said, beaming.

I pictured him sitting on top of a mountain of trash, flies buzzing around him, feet tapping on corncobs and banana peels as he tucked into his burger.

"What's the name of this restaurant again?" my dad asked.

"It's called Ray's Burgers, down in Carlsbad," Uncle Li said.

"The boss's name was Ray?" my dad asked.

"No. The boss's name was Yi-fung, but 'Ray's Burgers' sounds a lot better than 'Yi-fung's Burgers.' "

My dad chuckled. He pointed to the pen on the table. "Grab that pen, will ya, Mia? Write down Ray's Burgers."

"Yeah, tell your friends, that is one place you *never* want to work," Uncle Li said, reaching for another spring roll.

I went to my room and found an empty journal. In it, I wrote *Restaurant in Carlsbad, Ray's Burgers. Boss only feeds workers white on white on white.* I showed it to my dad.

"In *Chinese*," he said. "So we can all read it."

Underneath the English, I started writing in Chinese, stopping when I got to the word *burger.*

"How do you write *burger*?" I asked my mom.

My mom frowned, taking the pen from me. "Two years in America and she's nearly forgotten all her Chinese," she said apologetically to Uncle Li.

"Ah, English is more important anyway," he said, batting away her concern.

My mother sighed.

"That's the thing about moving kids from one country to another. They're not good at either language."

Her words sat on my shoulders, heavy as

rocks. I looked down at my feet and nearly jumped when my mother touched my hand.

"*But,* she does all the math at the front desk, don't you, honey?" she said, smiling at me.

CHAPTER 16

That night, I could not stop thinking about Uncle Li and how he was willing to do anything, go literally anywhere, even into the belly of a Dumpster, to get what he wanted. Was that insanity or courage?

I didn't know. What I did know was when they served us hamburgers at school the next day — REAL burgers, not saltine burgers — I was bringing mine home for Uncle Li. I didn't care how loudly my stomach protested.

Carefully, I wrapped the burger up and hid it in my jacket. I made sure not to squish it all day long. When I got home, I heated the burger up in the microwave, then rewrapped it in a napkin, just like they did in commercials on TV. I brought it to Uncle Li's room.

Uncle Li was delighted. He asked me whether I'd eaten, and I lied and said I had.

But then my stomach betrayed me and

growled loudly. Uncle Li laughed.

"C'mon, let's eat it together," he said.

I sat down and divided the burger. And this time, I shared more than just a couple of crumbs.

Uncle Li ended up staying three nights. Each night was filled with delicious food and riveting stories about customers and things like their weird sauce requests (one guy insisted on burgers with ketchup and jam). By the end of his stay, our refrigerator was nearly empty, so my mom and I went to Ralphs, the American grocery store three blocks away. Normally, we'd go to the Chinese supermarket, but today, there was a two-for-one cauliflower sale at Ralphs.

"We should really stop letting people stay at the motel for free," my mom said with a sigh. She picked up the cauliflowers, put them in a plastic bag, and tossed it into the cart.

"But you and Dad are so happy when they come," I said, thinking of how animated my parents were at dinner these last few days.

"I know. And they're such good people. And their stories?" She put her hand on her chest. "Heart-wrenching."

They really were. All week, I'd been going back in and filling in all the details in my journal. They were fascinating, the stories.

"But I'm worried about Mr. Yao," my mom groaned. "If he catches us . . ."

Her voice trailed off. I worried about that too sometimes. Mr. Yao hadn't come around for a week — we were due a visit anytime.

"We should be careful," I said, reaching for a box of Honey Nut Cheerios, my favorite.

"I think I just have to put my foot down and say, no more visitors," my mom said. She looked at the items in the shopping cart, eyes lingering on my Honey Nut Cheerios.

"What? I always get them," I said.

I picked up the box and held it close to my chest. I knew money was tight, but surely not no-Cheerios tight, right?

Right?

Her pause said it all.

"It's fine," she said, reaching for the box. "Here, put that back in the cart."

But I held on to it. I peered longingly at it, all those delicious honey-kissed circles on the box, the smiling bee that said *Nobody can say no to Honey Nut Cheerios!* Well, I can think of one person. Me.

Slowly, I put the box back up on the shelf.

"What are you doing?" my mom asked.

"It's okay," I said.

"You don't want it anymore?"

I shrugged. "I'm kind of sick of it."

I turned away before my mom could see my eyes.

That Sunday, as usual, my father and I loaded up the car with empty aluminum cans. You'd be amazed at how much soda people drank at the motel. My dad and I crushed the cans, put them into trash bags, and drove over to the local recycling center. I wished my mom could come too, but Mr. Yao had the rule about never leaving the motel unattended.

The recycling center gave us ten dollars for the cans, which we took and exchanged for pennies. Then we went over to the lake, where we sat and went over them, one by one, trying to find the one special penny we'd been on the lookout for as long as I can remember. It was the 1943 copper alloy penny. My dad said it was worth $40,000.

"At least!" my dad insisted. "Maybe even more!"

When he told me that, my mouth went dry — $40,000 for just one penny. Think of all the Honey Nut Cheerios we could buy!

My dad said that the reason they were so valuable was because there were just forty of them made. They were made by accident,

during the war when pennies were con-
verted to steel. So far, only one had been
found. The rest were just out there, waiting
to be found.

We didn't find the 1943 that day, but we
did find a 1984 double die and my dad said
that was worth thirty dollars. A doubled die
is when they accidentally print the words
twice on the coin. Anytime that kind of
mistake happens, the coin's automatically
worth a lot more.

I tilted my head to one side. "Why's it
automatically worth more?" I asked my dad.

He didn't respond right away, so I added
the 1984 doubled die to our collection of
"valuable" pennies. We had about seventeen
pennies in the bag from all our searching
over the years; altogether, it was worth
about $300. My dad was enormously proud
of them. He never once suggested we cash
in those pennies. They were his babies.

"Why are the mistake ones worth more,
Dad?"

"That's a great question," he said. He put
his coins down and turned to me. "The fact
that a penny can be worth four hundred
thousand times more because of a mistake,
what does that tell you?"

I shook my head.

"It means a mistake isn't always a mistake," he said. "Sometimes a mistake is actually an opportunity, but we just can't see it right then and there. Do you know what I mean?"

He gazed into the distance.

"Like coming to this country, for instance," he said. My dad shook his head and chuckled. "I thought . . . I thought it was going to be very different."

I closed my eyes, thinking of the plane ride over. My dad had given my hand a squeeze and asked, "Are you excited?" I nodded, even though I was more scared than excited. But he wasn't. He was just excited.

As we flew across the Pacific, he and my mom had talked a mile a minute, making plans and setting goals. My mother asked if he thought we could go see the Statue of Liberty.

"Sure! That'll be the first place we go for vacation — New York City!" my dad had said. "We'll stay in a nice hotel. Get dinner in a nice restaurant."

"You really think we can do all that?" my mom had asked.

"I *know* we can," my dad had said, beaming.

I looked at my father now, two years later. He had grays in his hair. The creases on his forehead had become ditches.

"Would you still have come?" I asked him softly. "If you knew?"

He looked up at me.

"In a heartbeat," he said. "You know why?"

I shook my head.

"Because of you. You're my special penny, Mia," he said, touching my nose. "You know that?"

I smiled. Just sitting next to my dad by the beautiful lake, it made me so happy. I decided right then and there it didn't even matter if we ever found the 1943.

(But it *would* be nice if we did.)

CHAPTER 17

My mom was hopping from one foot to the other in the front office when we got back from the lake. While we were gone, the cable stopped working. And that was a big problem, because free cable was a basic requirement of every motel. It was one of those things customers absolutely had to have.

"You gotta do something! I'm missing *Cheers*!" Fred exclaimed.

We picked up the phone and speed-dialed Mr. Yao. Luckily, even Mr. Yao understood the urgency of the situation — this was not like the washing machine breaking down. People could live with dirty towels for a day or two, but they *needed* their TV. He immediately dispatched his cable repairman to the motel, a guy named José.

José arrived at the motel half an hour later with a pickup truck full of tools and his daughter in tow. My jaw dropped to the ground when I saw who hopped out of the truck.

It was Lupe!

Lupe stood in the parking lot, squinting at the front office and blocking the sun from her eyes with her hands. I waved to her and started running outside. Her hands flew to her mouth when she saw me.

At first, neither of us said a word. We just stood awkwardly at the front desk as my parents cleaned and her dad fixed the cable up on the roof. I kept looking over at her, hoping she'd say something. Finally, when I couldn't stand it anymore, I cleared my throat.

"I have to tell you something," I said.

"What?" she asked.

"I don't really have a golden retriever," I admitted.

"I have to tell you something too," she said nervously.

"What?" I asked.

"Me neither," she said.

I smiled.

It turned out, just as I had been making everything up at school, so had Lupe. She didn't have a big house or three dogs, and although she did have a trampoline, it was one of those tiny ones and there was no way you could do a flip on it.

"I don't know why I said all those things," she said. "It just came out."

"I don't know why I said all those things either," I said.

The best part about Lupe and I coming clean was that she knew all about Mr. Yao and how horrible he was. She knew more than I did, in fact. She told me he had four motels in Los Angeles, one in San Diego, a couple in Nevada, and one on some island in Florida.

"That's why he's sometimes gone for weeks at a time," she explained.

Her dad had been working for him for years, and he was just as rotten to him as he was to us.

"So you know that Jason's his son?" I asked.

"Of course I know that Jason's his son," Lupe said. "Didn't I tell you from day one that he was terrible?"

I could hardly contain it. My heart swelled with excitement. Finally, I had someone to share all this with.

"You know what, Lupe?" I asked. "I hope our cable breaks down every day so you can come over."

"Me too." Lupe grinned.

CHAPTER 18

While Lupe's dad fixed the cable, I filled
Lupe in on all the things that had happened,
including Mr. Yao changing the deal on us,
the drunk man attacking me, and Mr. Yao
refusing to buy us a security camera.

"Oh, you'll never get Mr. Yao to buy that,"
Lupe said. "You're lucky if he pays the
electricity."

"But he has so much money! Have you
seen his house? It's enormous!" I said.

"Being rich doesn't mean you're gener-
ous. I've gone with my dad to some of the
nicest homes in LA. You should see some of
these rich people! They have so much
money, but they're *so* mean to us —"

"Just because we're poorer than them," I
finished the sentence.

Lupe looked at the floor.

"And because we're brown," she said quietly.

I looked down at our two arms, mine

golden like the desert sand, and hers warm like cinnamon.

"Well, when we're rich, we're not going to be that way," I said.

"We're going to have to get off the roller coaster first," Lupe said. I furrowed my eyebrows.

"What roller coaster?" I asked.

Lupe explained. According to her dad, there were two roller coasters in America — one for rich people and one for poor people. On the rich roller coaster, people have money, so their kids get to go to great schools. Then *they* grow up and make a lot of money, so *their* kids get to go to great schools.

"And 'round and 'round they go," Lupe said.

"And poor people?" I asked.

"We're on a different roller coaster. On our roller coaster, our parents don't have money, so we can't go to good schools, and then we can't get good jobs. So then *our* kids can't go to good schools, they can't get good jobs, and so on and so forth," Lupe said.

It was an incredibly depressing thought. The only nice thing about it was that Lupe used the word *we.*

"Sucks," she said.

It did suck. And she was right too. My parents bobbed along from one bad job to another. Sometimes, I even felt like I was on a roller coaster — I had the same queasy feeling in my tummy.

"But wait. What about Jason?" I asked.

"He goes to the same school as us."

"For now," she said. "But just wait. Come high school, he's going to go to a private school — for sure."

"That's good," I said. I wished he would go to private school now, somewhere far, far away.

Lupe shook her head.

"No, it's not," she said. "He'll learn all sorts of stuff that we don't know and we'll never be as successful."

I was curious what Lupe thought of as "successful." Everybody seemed to have different criteria. I used to think being successful meant having enough to eat, but now that I was getting free lunch at school, I wondered if I should set my standards higher.

When I asked Lupe, she put two fingers to her chin and thought real hard.

"I think being successful in this country means having a living room without a bed in it," she decided.

I immediately wanted to run over and

cover up my parents' bed in the living room so she wouldn't see it. But Lupe spotted where I was looking and quickly added, "It's okay! Actually, you can think of the *front office* as being sort of like your living room."

I nodded.

"Right," I said.

It was really nice of Lupe to say that, but I knew it wasn't the truth. The living room was the living room and there was clearly a bed in ours, which meant we weren't successful in this country. Not yet anyway. We *had* to get off the bad roller coaster and onto the good one.

Chapter 19

Lupe and I became inseparable. Whereas before, we were best friends bound by lies, now we shared a secret truth. I stopped pretending that I always wore long pants and long sleeves — even on days when it was 102 — because I was always cold (the real reason was because sunscreen was too expensive). Or that I was saving my cookie from lunch for after PE (when really I was saving it for my parents). She stopped pretending she hated sports (turns out, she also had no medical insurance). She and her family were immigrants too. They'd come over from Mexico when she was three. We told each other everything.

Well, not *everything.* I didn't tell her my dad sometimes let people stay at the motel for free. It wasn't that I thought Lupe would tell on us, I just thought some things were better kept as secrets. Kind of like the security camera we didn't have, even though the sign said we did.

One day, while doing my math homework, I had to answer a question about how much money a flower shop made in a month. It was a fairly basic question, and I solved it no problem. But it got me thinking. How much money did the Calivista make? I'd never actually calculated before.

Curious, I pulled out the ledger from the bottom drawer of the front desk. The ledger was this big black book my dad kept with meticulous records of how many customers we had each day.

I ran my fingers over the names of the customers. On any given day at the Calivista, we had about twenty customers, including the weeklies. Mr. Yao kept the first fifteen, as per his revised deal, and my parents got five dollars per person for the other five. But *say* we got to keep all twenty dollars per customer, and didn't have to share with evil Mr. Yao — how much would we make?

I lined the numbers up neatly on my paper and started doing the math. My eyes boggled at the numbers: $12,000. That's how much we made for Mr. Yao last month.

My parents, on the other hand, only got $750. At that rate, it would take them over a year to make what Mr. Yao made in just one month! Mr. Yao wasn't on just any old rich roller coaster, he was on one of those crazy, upside-down, hair-raising, scream-your-head-off roller coasters. And we were the people operating it for him.

Of course, he did own the place. And he had to pay for electricity and stuff. But still.

The next day at school, I went to the library.

"Can I help you?" Mrs. Matthews, the librarian, asked as she looked up from a reference book.

"I want to look up the price of buying a motel," I said.

Mrs. Matthews raised a sharp eyebrow.

"It's for a . . . math project," I quickly added.

"I see," she said. She turned back to her computer and started typing. "All right, let's see what we can find. . . ."

She drummed her fingers on her desk as she waited for the computer to load. "Looks like a motel costs anywhere between three hundred thousand dollars to a million dollars."

"Did you say a *million* dollars?"

Mrs. Matthews nodded.

"Yup," Mrs. Matthews said. "Even more for some of the nicer ones."

Well, that did it. There's no way we could

ever buy a roller coaster.

"Oh, look," Mrs. Matthews said, chuckling at the computer.

"What is it?"

"There's an old couple in Vermont looking to give away their motel. Says here they're holding an essay contest to determine who to give it to," Mrs. Matthew said. "Isn't that sweet?"

"Can you . . . uh . . ." I swallowed hard. My heart was beating so fast, I could hardly get the words out. "Can you print that out for me?"

Over and over again, I read the words. A couple in Vermont wanted to give their motel away. They'd been running it for years and now they were both in their seventies. Instead of selling it, they were holding an essay contest. The deadline was not until after Thanksgiving. There was an entry fee, though, and it wasn't cheap — $300. But *look* at the essay topic: "What would you do if you owned a motel?"

This was it! This was our ticket onto the good roller coaster!

Carefully, I hid the piece of paper inside a library book and smuggled it back to class. I didn't want my classmates to see it: $300 was nothing to them, and a bunch of them were probably great writers. If they saw it, they'd all want to enter and then I'd be doomed.

I clutched the book tightly with both hands and walked back to class, passing Lupe on the way to my seat. I slid into my seat and glanced over at her. She arched her eyebrows (*What's up?*) and I shrugged my shoulders (*Nothing much*).

"All right, kids, listen up," Mrs. Douglas said. "Today we're going to learn about China."

A boy behind me raised his hand.

"Yes, Stuart?"

"Is China in Japan?" Stuart asked.

Jason turned around and glared at him. "No, idiot, it's not in Japan."

Stuart shriveled in his seat. "Well, where's China, then?" he asked.

"In China!" Jason said.

"Oh."

Mrs. Douglas told Jason and Stuart both to hush, and she started talking about the imperial era and Qin Shi Huang, the first emperor of China. She showed us a picture of Qin Shi Huang. I don't know where Mrs. Douglas got her picture from, but in the picture, Qin Shi Huang's eyes were ridiculously slanted. His eyebrows went all the way up to his forehead.

The kids in the front row couldn't stop cracking up. Every time Mrs. Douglas wrote something on the board, they would turn around and make slanted eyes at me and Jason. This prompted Jason to raise his hand.

"Excuse me, Mrs. Douglas," he said. "I'd just like to clarify I'm not Chinese; I'm Taiwanese."

"Ohhh . . . kay," Mrs. Douglas said.

Stuart raised his hand again.

"Is *that* in Japan?" he asked.

"No, you moron!" Jason yelled. "That's not in Japan either!"

As Mrs. Douglas reprimanded Jason for calling Stuart a moron, I sat very quietly in my seat. I knew I should have felt glad that Jason clarified to everyone that he was not the same as me, but I couldn't help but feel a little sad too. Because now, when the kids in the first row turned around, they only made slanted eyes at me.

CHAPTER 20

I ran up the stairs two at a time, holding the book from the library, the one with the essay contest printed out in it. I couldn't wait to tell my parents.

Before I could open my mouth, my mother looked at my book and frowned.

"*Another* new book?" she said. "You should be spending more time doing math. Something you can actually get good at." Then she became all nostalgic. "You know when I was your age, I used to eavesdrop on my brother's math lessons. . . ."

Yeah, yeah, yeah. I didn't have time for this.

"I'm not you, Mom," I exclaimed. The words came shooting out of my mouth, and my mom flinched. "I'm sorry. I just mean . . . Maybe I like something else."

"Like what?" she asked. She put her broom down and crossed her arms.

I bit my lip.

"Like writing?"

"English writing?" she asked, like it was the most preposterous thing in the world, like I'd just said basket weaving.

I nodded.

"You heard Mr. Yao. You gotta be *native* at English. And I'm sorry, but we're just not."

Mr. Yao? Since when was he an expert on anything other than meanness?

"You can, however, be native at math."

"I don't want to be native at math. . . ."

My mom frowned.

"You're not getting it, are you?" she said. She sat down on the bed and looked me in the eye. "You just can't be as good as the white kids in their language, honey. It's *their* language."

My gaze sank to the floor.

As I dragged myself out of the room, my mother called after me, "Someday you'll thank me!"

She's wrong, I told myself.

She was wrong to the power of infinity.

I thought about picking up the phone to call Lupe, but instead, I flipped on the TV. A rerun of *The Simpsons* was playing. I stared at Marge Simpson, with her big hair and easygoing smile. Marge, to me, was like the perfect American mom. So warm and forgiving that even if Bart was setting the house on fire, she'd continue chatting with her sisters on the phone. "Maybe he just needs more love," she'd say.

Sometimes, I wondered what it would be like to have an American mom. Just for a day. I could eat all the chocolate chip cookies I wanted because American moms on TV were always baking them. Or making casseroles. Or organizing birthday parties with themes.

I'll tell you what they were *not* doing. They weren't pestering their kids to do more math.

Whatever. I'd show her. She didn't even have to know about the essay contest. One day, it'd just be like, "Hey, can you pass the chopsticks? Oh, and by the way, I won a motel."

Mr. Yao's car roared into the motel and interrupted my daydreaming. I flipped off the TV as he and Jason walked up to the front office.

"It's important, son, that you understand every part of the family business," Mr. Yao said to Jason as they stepped in.

"But I don't understand why we have to do this now," Jason protested.

"Do what now?" I asked.

Mr. Yao lifted up the front desk divider so

that he and Jason could join me behind the desk.

"Today, Jason's going to do your job," Mr. Yao announced. "He's going to check customers in."

You've got to be kidding me.

Jason was not a natural checker-iner. For one, he didn't have good customer service skills like me — no surprise there. But he also had basic problems figuring out the math.

"So it's twenty dollars a night, plus tax," he told a customer while his father watched and I stood behind them.

The customer gave him a hundred-dollar bill and wanted change.

Jason struggled to calculate the tax, which in Anaheim, California, was 13 percent.

"Uhhh, do you have a calculator?" he asked me.

"It's twenty-two dollars and sixty cents," I told him. I'd checked so many people in by now, $22.60 was tattooed in my head.

"Don't forget, I need two rooms," the customer reminded him.

"Right," Jason said. He pulled out his hand and tried to do the math in the air with his fingers. "So that's . . ."

"Two times twenty-two sixty?" Mr. Yao

yelled. "You can't figure out what that is?"

"Hang on — just give me a second," Jason said. He bit his lip. "You gotta carry the one . . . and then add the —"

Mr. Yao shook his head and stomped into the manager's quarters.

After Jason finally figured out the math and gave the customer his keys, we went to find his father. He was in the kitchen.

"I did it! I checked in my first customer," Jason told his dad proudly.

His father didn't say anything.

"Well? How'd I do?" Jason asked.

Mr. Yao breathed in and out, looking like he was trying to contain a wildfire. And was failing.

"How'd you do? You were awful. A disgrace. All that using your fingers to do math — what are you, five?"

Jason's face turned beet red.

"Your math isn't even as good as the *girl's,*" Mr. Yao spat the words at him as he eyed Jason up and down. "God, you embarrass me."

"It was his first time," I said in Jason's defense.

"Yeah, well, he screwed up!" Mr. Yao growled. He stared at Jason long and hard to make sure his words sank in. I looked down. I could see the whites of Jason's knuckles.

Afterward, when Mr. Yao went out to talk to my parents, I walked over to Jason. He was sitting all by himself in a corner in the front office.

I knew exactly what he was feeling because I had felt it just a couple of hours ago when my mom yelled at me.

"It's okay," I said softly.

Jason shook his head.

"Don't," he said.

I put my hand on his shoulder anyway.

He jerked his body away.

"Just don't."

CHAPTER 21

Pounding woke us up at dawn the next day. Earsplitting pounding like someone was attacking the front office door with a jackhammer. I jumped out of bed.

Mr. Lorenz, one of the customers from the night before, was standing in front of the front office. Quickly, my dad buzzed him in.

"My car!" Mr. Lorenz shrieked. "It's gone!"

Mr. Lorenz's neon-green Ford Thunderbird had been taken in the middle of the night. He had parked it right in front of his room, room 5, and when he woke up, it was gone.

"We have to find out who did this!" I said, turning to my parents. "You think it was one of the other customers?"

I immediately grabbed the customer logbook to see who stayed here last night.

"Could have been anybody," Mr. Lorenz

said. "Somebody could have come in here in the middle of the night and taken off with my car."

I made a mental note to add "parking lot gate" to my wish list.

My father picked up the phone.

"Hello? Mr. Yao?" my dad said. "Something terrible has happened."

Mr. Yao arrived half an hour later. "How could this happen?" he said to my mom and dad, gesturing angrily with his hands.

"We don't know," my dad said. "We're just as surprised as you!"

Mr. Yao picked up the phone and called the police. After that, he went around from room to room, waking up all the customers.

"Have you seen a green Ford Thunderbird?" he asked them, peering suspiciously into their rooms.

One of the guests said he did hear some noise at around 3:00 a.m., like someone was trying to start their car.

Mr. Yao turned to my dad.

"Did you see anybody leave at three a.m.?" he asked.

My dad sheepishly admitted that he didn't know, he had been sleeping, to which Mr. Yao frowned and said, "Stop sleeping!"

Mr. Yao then asked us if there were any customers who left without checking out. My dad and I went to check if anyone had gone in the middle of the night, and sure enough, when we went around, we found five keys. We gave Mr. Yao the numbers of the rooms and the names of the customers.

Mr. Yao wanted to know what the customers looked like. I tried to describe them the best I could.

"Let's see, Mr. Roberto had a mustache," I said. "But it wasn't one of those long archy ones. It was a small and tidy one. And Mrs. Robinson, she was about the same height as my mom, a little taller."

I closed my eyes trying to recall any other details about her.

"She had long, curly black hair, past her shoulders, not in braids like some other black women," I said. Mr. Yao's eyes bulged.

"Wait a minute, she's *black*?" he yelled. "I thought I told you not to rent to bad people!"

My throat went dry. I could hear the sound of my breathing, hard and fast. "You said *bad* people, not black people."

"Any idiot knows — black people are dangerous," Mr. Yao said.

"That's not true!" I was stunned. "Hank's not dangerous. For one." I narrowed my eyes at Mr. Yao. "*You're* the one who's dangerous."

"Mia," my dad said. Nervously, my dad turned to Mr. Yao. "Sir, we can't judge someone based on their skin color. It isn't right. This is America."

Mr. Yao snorted.

"If you really believe that, you're even dumber than I thought," he said. "Clearly you have no idea how this country really works."

The sound of police cars pulling in made us look up.

"What's going on here?" the police officers asked when they stepped in. There were two officers, both male and white. They had lots of things on their uniforms, sticks hanging from their belt, radios, and walkie-talkies, which they talked into as they walked up to the front desk. And guns.

I stared at their guns.

Mr. Yao quickly filled them in on what happened. From the familiar way they talked with him, it seemed like they knew him. I wondered if the cops had been at the Calivista before. Mr. Yao handed them the list of customers who had left in the middle of the night. He told them he thought it was Mrs. Robinson who stole Mr. Lorenz's car. He went so far as to circle Mrs. Robinson's name and write the word *black* next to it.

"And where is Mrs. Robinson now?" the officers asked.

"She left, but I really don't think —" I started to say.

The officers cut me off with a sharp *shhh*. They only wanted to hear from Mr. Yao.

Mr. Yao proceeded to tell the officers about the other customers. They seemed particularly interested in hearing about the weeklies.

"Are they home? Can we interview them?"

"Absolutely," Mr. Yao said, leading the way outside.

The weeklies were outside talking about what happened. At the sight of Mr. Yao walking over, Hank quickly moved his tomato plant into his room. Mr. Yao did not like Hank growing plants outside his room. He said Hank hadn't rented that space.

The cops walked up to the weeklies.

"We'd like to ask you guys some questions," the cops said. "How long have you been living here?"

"About three months," Billy Bob said. "I was staying over at Days before."

One of the officers turned to Hank and asked, "And you?"

"About six months," Hank told him.

The officer jotted it down.

"Do you have a job?" he asked Hank.

"Yeah. I work over at the gas station on Orange and Knott," he said.

"What's this about?" Fred asked. "You think *we* did it?"

Mrs. Q put a hand to her chest and let out a shrill "Good God!"

"Sir, ma'am, we're not saying that. We're just asking questions," the cop said.

"But you're asking the wrong people!" I interjected.

They ignored me. As they carried on interrogating the weeklies, I kept trying to interrupt. But every time I tugged on their shirt, the police officers said, "Please don't touch me."

Finally, they told the weeklies they could all go back to their rooms.

As the weeklies started walking back to their rooms, one of the officers pulled Hank aside.

"Except for you," he said.

"Why me?" Hank asked.

"Because I said so," the cop said, staring Hank down. The weeklies looked at Hank, and Hank looked at them. Then he nodded and told them to go on without him.

After the other weeklies left, both cops turned their attention back to Hank.

"Now. Where were we? You said you work at Orange and Knott," the commanding officer said, turning to the other cop. "Orange and Knott. Let's check that out."

He looked at Hank again.

"Have you been having any financial difficulties lately?" he asked.

"Excuse me?" Hank asked.

"Have you needed to borrow any money?"

"No."

"Have you sold anything in the last ten weeks?"

The cops suddenly turned their attention to me.

"Do people ever come over looking for him? Does he ever ask you to hold something for him? Doesn't have to be big . . ."

I shook my head. "No."

The officer seemed displeased with my answer and frowned. "I'm sorry. I'm going to need you to go back inside with your parents."

"Hank's a good guy!" I yelled as the officer took my arm and dragged me away.

The whole time, I looked back at Hank, at the frustration and fury in his eyes, as he said the words over and over, "I didn't do it!"

I sat with my nose pressed up against the

window, watching the police interrogate Hank. Several times, I ran outside, only to be escorted back in.

"See? The police know I'm right," Mr. Yao said, taking their interrogation of Hank as evidence that his theory about black people was valid. He was wrong. The only thing it proved was that the police were just like him.

I counted the minutes until he and his racist thoughts would finally leave. Surprisingly, the person who remained most calm throughout the incident was Mr. Lorenz. It sounded like he had car insurance and he figured he could get the money back that way.

At half past noon, the cops finally stopped interrogating Hank and got back in their cars. They didn't have enough evidence to make an arrest (because he didn't do it — duh), but they said they'd be back.

"You'll hear from us again real soon," the commanding officer, Officer Phillips, said, looking at all of us. His eyes lingered especially long on Hank before he turned away.

After the cops and Mr. Yao finally left, I went over to Hank's room.

Hank was sitting in his chair, slumped over like a half-filled sack. He looked absolutely exhausted.

I walked over and put my hand on his shoulder.

"I'm so sorry you had to go through that."

"It's all right," he said.

"It's not all right! They were awful. They just assumed you did it! How could they think that?"

The more I thought about it, the more riled up I got. But Hank just sat there, quiet and unfazed, gazing in the general direction of the pool. The sun burned through the window. I could see little tiny particles of dust floating in his room.

"Why are you not more upset?" I asked him.

He shrugged.

"Guess I'm just used to it," he said. "This kind of thing happens to me all the time."

"It does?"

He nodded. "To all black people in this country. In some way or the other."

He dropped his head into his hands. I sat very still, thinking about what he said. I could hear the faint honking of cars, a couple laughing in the room next to us. I wanted to scream *Stop!* Stop honking. Stop laughing. How can it be business as usual when this was happening to people like Hank?

Hank got up and went to wash his face. When he returned, he was holding a pack of Oreos. As he set the Oreos down onto his little table, I stared at the cookies and thought about the world of difference there was between the two colors.

CHAPTER 22

I sat at my desk with my hand over my tummy, not hearing a word Mrs. Douglas was saying. Wave after wave of nausea hit me every time I thought about the day before, the words Mr. Yao said, the words the cops said. I tried to drown them out, but they kept coming back.

Jason turned to me and said, "Hey. Meet me at the auditorium during recess."

I looked over at him. Sometimes I forgot how much he was the spitting image of his father.

"Please," Jason said. "It's important."

I was about to shake my head, but there was an urgency in his eyes I'd never seen before. Did his dad tell him what happened? Was that why he needed to talk to me — so he could apologize?

At recess, I walked over to the auditorium. Jason was already inside waiting for me. He smiled when he saw me come in. He was

holding something behind his back —
dandelions, which he presented to me.

"These are for you," he said, stretching
out his arm. I stared at the flowers, so warm
and bright in my downcast hands. "You like
them?" he asked.

I nodded slowly.

"Good," Jason said, relieved.

"But what I really want is for your dad
—"

"I know! I'm going to tell him! As soon as
he gets back from his business trip, I'm going to tell him," Jason said.

I nodded. Good for him for finally standing up to his dad.

"I don't care what he says," Jason said.
"He needs to know how much I like you!"

I stopped nodding.

"Wait, what?" I asked.

He grabbed my arms and looked into my
eyes.

"I like you, Mia," he said again.

I shook my head. No. NO!

"I didn't want to believe it myself. I was
like, how is this possible?" Jason rattled on
a mile a minute. "But it's true. Whenever
I'm around you, Mia, I get this tingly feeling. . . ."

My insides twisted and turned. A slimy
snake was zigzagging through me. The more

Jason described, the more I squirmed.

"This isn't happening," I said, squeezing my eyes shut. I could feel my breakfast at the base of my throat.

"Oh, it's happening," he said. "And it's going to be great —"

I turned to him.

"JASON, I DON'T LIKE YOU!" I exploded.

Jason looked like he'd been punched.

"But . . . but . . . you said you liked the flowers. You said you wanted me to tell my dad. . . ."

"I thought you were talking about your dad being racist!"

Jason took a step back. "My dad's not racist," he said.

"Yes, he is." I gasped to fill my lungs. "He's racist."

"Shut up!" Jason yelled.

"No, you shut up!" I looked at him hard. "I could never like you. Never! Not even if you were the last boy on earth. I'd rather like a rock."

He turned and ran.

I stood in the auditorium listening to the echo of my words, feeling a tiny bit mean. Yet 100 percent relieved.

Jason didn't come back to class after recess.

When I asked, Mrs. Douglas said he wasn't feeling well and had to go home. Lupe immediately started poking me and asking me what happened, and when I finally told her, she wasn't even surprised.

"It makes sense," she said. "I mean, you're both Chinese."

How did *that* make sense? Just because we're both Chinese, we're supposed to like each other? What about the fact that he's evil and I'm not?

"Maybe it's a good thing," Lupe said. "Maybe his dad will be nicer to your family from now on."

I shook my head at her. The way I shot him down, there was no going nice after that.

There was only going nuclear.

CHAPTER 23

Hank was waiting for me at the motel when I got back from school.

"What are you doing home so early?" I asked him. Usually, he didn't get home until well past six.

"The cops came around to the gas station. They started asking me questions, asking my employer," he said.

"And?" I asked him. He stared into the tiny lines of the front desk wood.

"And my boss freaked out and fired me."

I felt the floor beneath me open up and swallow me whole.

"*What?* But you didn't do anything wrong!"

"Doesn't matter. The boss said it was bad for business having the cops poke around." Hank pulled out a crumpled hundred-dollar bill from his pocket and slid it across the desk.

"This here's my last paycheck," he said.

I looked at the bill on the table.

"What are you going to do?" I asked him.

He didn't say anything. He just gazed out the window at the leaves in the pool.

"Hank!" I said loudly. "You have to fight this!"

Hank shook his head.

"You don't get it, kid," he said. "I've been fighting my whole life. I'm done. It's no use fighting — people are gonna be the way they're gonna be."

After Hank went back to his room, I searched the kitchen for canned foods. If that was his last paycheck and he'd just given it to us, he was going to need all the help he could get. I was in the middle of rummaging through our fridge when I heard a knock on the door. It was the security guard from the Topaz Inn two doors down, a Chinese guy about my parents' age, probably second or third generation from the confident way he spoke English.

"Open up, I gotta talk to you!" he hollered.

I buzzed him in.

"Heard you guys got a little visit from the cops," he said. A sly grin stretched across his face.

The Topaz Inn people did not like us, and we didn't like them. To say that we had a little rivalry was an understatement. Every day, they tried to undercut our prices. They had a bigger motel, so naturally they had more rooms. But we had a better location, being the first motel on our block. You had to drive past us to get to Topaz Inn, which drove them nuts.

The Topaz people came up with all kinds of ridiculous tactics to get back at us, including one time when they had one of their people stand a few blocks up with a sign that said *Don't stay at the Calivista. It's full of roaches. Stay at the Topaz!* Mr. Yao happened to be driving by that day. When he saw what they were doing, he went straight to Ralphs, bought a dozen eggs, and hurled them at the sign. So it was a quite a shock to see the Topaz security guard standing here in our lobby.

"What do you want?" I asked him.

"Look, I know we've had our differences over the years," he said. "But in light of what's happened, I've come to offer a truce."

I stared at him.

"A truce?"

He nodded.

"What happened over here last night was

143

a tragedy," he said. "We were so upset when we heard about it."

"Really?" I said. I would have thought they'd be celebrating.

"Really," he said. "Now look. It's in neither of our interests if bad people stay at our motels. It gives the area a terrible rep and business suffers. So why don't we do this . . . ?"

He pulled out a piece of paper.

"This here is a list of all the bad people we've checked in the last month," he said.

I peered curiously at his list.

"I'm sure you have a few names of your own you'd like to add to it," he said.

I did, starting with the drunk guy.

"So here's what we're going to do. You tell me the names of your bad people and I'll tell you the names of our bad people. I'm going to show the list to the Lagoon Motel people and the other stores on our street, so we're all in on it. And if anybody from the list calls looking for a room, we'll tell them the same thing. No vacancy. How's that?"

I nodded. It sounded like a plan. I thought back to all the things that had happened these last few weeks. We could sure use more safety around here.

"All righty, then," he said. He took out his pen, and I took out my dad's big ledger with

144

all the customers' names and information.

"Ready?" he asked.

"Ready," I said.

He grinned, revealing a mouthful of very yellow teeth.

"Let's start with last month. Give me the names of all the black customers who have come through here in the last month," he said.

I slammed the ledger shut.

"Get out," I said, pointing at the door.

"Hey! No need to get worked up!" he said, holding his hands up. "I'm just trying to help!"

"Get *out!*" I repeated.

"Suit yourself," he huffed as he walked out, stuffing his list into his pocket. "But don't come crying to me when this place gets robbed again, which it *will.*"

CHAPTER 24

I rocked back and forth with the ledger in my arms, waiting for Lupe. I'd called her as soon as the awful security guard left. As her dad's car pulled in, the air howled of a coming storm.

"We have got to sneak over there and grab those lists," I said to Lupe. I couldn't wait to rip them to shreds.

Lupe shook her head. She plopped down at the front desk.

"That won't do any good," she said. "We'd get caught, and besides, the stores probably already have copies."

Lupe helped herself to a blank piece of white paper from the fax machine and started drawing with a pencil. Lupe was always drawing — buildings, people, dogs, cats, mountains, and, most of all, trees. She loved trees.

"Will you stop drawing?" I all but shouted at her.

Lupe put her pencil down and gave me a look. "The thing about prejudice is you can't *tell* people not to be prejudiced. You've got to show them. It's like writing."

I thought back to what Mrs. Douglas was always saying — you gotta show, not tell.

"Why can't you tell people?" I asked.

"Because they won't listen. It'll go in one ear and out the other," she said.

"So how do we show them?" I asked.

She pointed to the ledger still in my arms. "Who was here that night?" she asked. "Does it say in there?"

I opened up the ledger to the day that the car got stolen and ran my fingers down the list of customers. There were five customers who left in the middle of the night. They were:

Peter Orviati
Rebecca Thompson
Tommy Smith
Javier Roberto
Loretta Robinson

Next to their names, we'd copied down all their permanent addresses so that in case they left something, I could mail it back to them. The addresses sprawled as far south as San Diego and as far north as Sacramento.

"Have the police checked out these addresses yet?" Lupe asked.

I shook my head. To my knowledge, they didn't even have them.

"Well, what are you waiting for?" Lupe asked. "Call them up!"

"The customers?"

"No, the police."

My eyes widened. We'd never called the police before, not even on the day that the car got stolen. Mr. Yao had been the one who called.

Back in China, I had fond memories of the policemen. We used to call them uncle too. They'd help the elderly cross the road and find their way home if they got lost. I'm not even sure if they had guns. We'd sing songs in school about them, songs like, "If I was walking down the street and I found a penny, I'd give it to Uncle Policeman."

Things were different here. Here, the policemen had guns. And if you found a penny, I'm pretty sure you'd keep it. I know my dad and I would.

I went over to the drawer under the phone system and retrieved the card Officer Phillips gave us. He was the officer in charge of

148

the case. I picked up the phone, dialed the number, and handed the receiver to Lupe.

"You talk," I told her.

Lupe pushed the receiver away hard.

"No. This is your motel. You need to talk," she said.

Hesitantly, I put the receiver up to my ear. Officer Phillips picked up on the fourth ring.

"Hi, Officer Phillips, it's, uh . . . Mia Tang calling from the Calivista Motel," I said.

"The what?"

"The Calivista. You know, the motel where the car was stolen the other day," I said.

"Listen, kid, I've got a lot of work to do," he said. He sounded really annoyed to hear from me.

I looked at Lupe, who nudged me to go on.

"I just wanted to ask you if you've looked into all the customers that left early that night? I have all their home addresses here. I can give them to you right now if you like," I said.

"Will you let us just do our jobs, kid?" he said. "We already have a strong lead."

"You mean Hank?" I said. "He didn't do it!" How many times did I have to keep saying it? "And by the way, did you know you guys got him fired from his job?"

"He recently got fired from his job?" Officer Phillips's voice perked up. "That explains why he needed the money!"

"No. *You guys* got him fired. His boss saw you guys asking him questions and fired him," I told him. "Now he doesn't have a job."

There was silence on the other end. I looked over at Lupe.

"Well, that's unfortunate," Officer Phillips said. "But I'm sure there was more to it than that."

I shook my head into the phone. "No, there wasn't."

"Look, I really have work to do," he said.

"So that's it, then? You're just going to give up? You're not even going to look into the addresses?" I asked him.

"We're not *giving up.* We just have more pressing cases to deal with at the moment, involving armed robbery."

"And what about Mr. Lorenz? What's he supposed to do?"

"Oh, he's fine. I talked to him the other day. Already filed the claim with his insurance. Gonna get his money in thirty days. The good thing about this case is nobody got hurt," said Officer Phillips. And with that, he hung up the phone.

Yeah, nobody. Except Hank. I stared at the phone in my hand. I couldn't believe that Officer Phillips.

"We have to call his manager," I told Lupe. "He must have a manager."

Lupe shook her head. "It doesn't sound like this is top priority for them."

"Well, it should be!"

"You'd think."

"What should we do?" I looked down at the list of addresses. "We can't go to all these places by ourselves."

"Maybe the car will turn up," Lupe said. "Maybe someone will see it and put in a call."

Maybe.

CHAPTER 25

As Lupe was leaving the motel, a car pulled in and someone got out. My dad and I went out to greet her — it was another immigrant. My mother's face softened when she saw it was a woman this time.

Aunt Ling was a friend of Uncle Li's, and she was so famished, she practically inhaled the dumplings my mother made at dinner.

"Eat up. There's plenty here," my mother said, even though I knew that wasn't really true.

In between bites, the woman told us where she'd been working — at a nail salon down in Irvine, California.

"Irvine," my dad said. "That's supposed to be nice."

"Isn't that by the beach?" my mom asked.

"Well, I never got to see it," Aunt Ling said. "I spent the entire time hunched over, kneeling on the floor."

She told us how she would hold the hands

of wealthy American women as they complained right in front of her, about their Chinese maids and how they were probably taking things because "don't they all steal?"

"It was like I wasn't even there. They didn't even see me," she said. "I was just a nail clipper to them."

My mother reached for Aunt Ling's hand. "Well, we see you," she said.

My mother and I led Aunt Ling over to room 1, our best room. Aunt Ling was so touched by our hospitality, the next day, she insisted on doing my mother's nails.

"Oh, that's very nice of you, but it's not necessary," my mother said bashfully, tucking her hands under her armpit to hide them from Aunt Ling.

"Let me see," Aunt Ling insisted. "Don't be shy."

"Yeah, Mom, c'mon, let's see," I said.

Reluctantly, my mom put her hands out in front. We gasped. My mother's once shiny, smooth fingernails were now dry, yellow, and rough. The cleaning supplies she used every day to clean the rooms must have somehow seeped through her gloves and into her nails. Her nails were practically melting off her hands.

"It's been like this for weeks," my mom said, tears coming to her eyes. "I don't know what to do. It's all that Ajax and bleach!"

"Don't panic. I know just the thing!" Aunt Ling said. She got up and went into the kitchen, where she grabbed a cut-up lemon from the fridge and baking soda from the cupboard.

Next, she filled two bowls of warm water. She put the baking soda in the bowls and soaked my mom's hands in them. After half an hour, she lifted each hand up and scrubbed the nails with the lemon. I watched as she worked, scrubbing and drying, polishing and cleaning. When she was finally done, the nails looked transformed. She was able to get rid of most of the roughness, and what she couldn't get off, she covered up with a coat of glossy red nail polish. My mom was beaming.

"Quick. Take a picture!" my mom said.

I smiled and kneeled down before her and Aunt Ling. I pretend-clicked with my finger as my mother held her beautifully manicured hands out to the "camera."

"Eggplant!" I said.

As we waited for my mother's nail polish to dry, I asked Aunt Ling where she was heading to next.

"Sacramento," she announced. "There are some new nail salons opening up there."

"You're going to Sacramento?" I asked.

One of the addresses from that ledger was in Sacramento. I leaped out of my chair and raced over to the front desk to get the ledger.

"Can you do me a favor? Can you swing by this address? I need you to check something for me!"

Aunt Ling promised she'd go by the address when she got up to Sacramento. If the Thunderbird were there, she'd call me right away. Before she left, she asked my mom whether she could tell any of her friends about the Calivista.

"They could really use a place to stay. Their boss gave them the boot, and they're living out of their cars," she said.

"Oh, that's hard," my mom said, grimacing. "We've been there."

My parents exchanged a look. "The only thing is our boss, Mr. Yao . . ." my dad said, "he lives right here in Anaheim."

"Sometimes he doesn't come for weeks, though," I reminded them. "He has motels all over the place."

Aunt Ling put a well-manicured finger to her chin. "You know what would be great? If you guys had a sign or something for when he's here," she thought out loud.

"You mean a don't-come-in sign?" I chuckled.

"Yeah, but not something he'd understand," she said. "A secret sign that only *we* understand."

I looked around the front desk. My eyes fell on an old blue Yankees baseball cap. I picked it up.

"How about this?" I asked Aunt Ling. Her eyes widened.

"Yes!" she exclaimed. "That's perfect!"

CHAPTER 26

It was agreed that from now on, if we put the blue hat on the front desk, it meant don't come in — Mr. Yao's there. And no hat meant come on in.

We all shook hands on the new system and Aunt Ling got into her car and drove off. I hoped she would tell all her friends and we would soon get lots of visitors — visitors who were heading in the direction of the four remaining addresses.

Lupe was delighted to hear I was marching forward with my plan to "show, not tell." She came over again the next day after school. The two of us sat at the front desk, where as usual, she proceeded to draw trees.

"Why are you always drawing those things?" I asked her.

Lupe didn't look up. Her eyes were completely focused on the page. Today, she was drawing a massive oak with tiny little lines in the trunk.

"I like trees," she said, shading in the bark.

She didn't just like trees. She was obsessed with drawing them and was really good at it too. There was so much detail in her creations — hundreds of twigs and branches and leaves, which she would labor over for hours.

She pulled out a blank piece of paper from the fax machine.

"Here, I'll teach you," she said.

I looked at her, wary. I wasn't exactly what you call artistic. My idea of a good portrait was a smiley face with sunglasses.

"You want to start off with the trunk," she said, pointing to my paper.

I did as I was told and drew two thick lines for my trunk.

"Not so straight," she said. She took her pencil and started making little vertical lines, lumps, and curves in my trunk.

"No tree is perfect, remember that," she said. "That's what gives it character."

I smiled at Lupe and how grown-up she sounded. It was one of the things I liked the most about her. She showed me how to add branches to my trunk. According to her, the easiest way to draw branches and twigs was to make lots and lots of tiny little *v*'s.

It was hard work making all those little

v's and I got a little impatient, so I started shading in my tree, eager to get on with it.

"Don't rush!" Lupe said, frowning at my shading and pointing to the tiny little twigs on her own tree. "See, it's all in the detail."

We worked side by side for an hour, neither of us saying anything except occasionally to borrow the eraser. So deep were we into our drawings that we nearly jumped when Hank came and knocked on the door. I buzzed him in.

"Hey, can I have Mr. Yao's number?" Hank asked.

"What for?" I asked him.

"Didn't you say he had all those other motels? Maybe he needs a handyman," Hank said.

"You want to ask *Mr. Yao* for a job?" I asked. I glanced at Lupe. "But . . ."

"But what?" Hank asked. He leaned in to me. "C'mon, Mia, I'm desperate."

I wanted to tell him it didn't matter how desperate he was, Mr. Yao was not going to go for it. Not after all the horrible things he said that night when the car got stolen.

But then I looked into Hank's eyes. He was the one who first warned me about Mr. Yao. There's no way he would be asking me this if he had any other option. So I dialed the number and handed him the phone.

"It's ringing," I told him.

As Hank picked up the phone and started talking to Mr. Yao, Lupe and I hopped off our stools and went to my room. Gently, I picked up the extension.

"Hi, Mr. Yao? It's Hank Caleb calling from the Calivista," Hank said.

"What do you want?" Mr. Yao asked, barely hiding the irritation in his voice.

"I just want to call you to see if you might need a handyman at one of your motels," Hank said.

"Why? You know somebody?" Mr. Yao asked.

"Yeah. Me," Hank told him. "I spent a summer painting houses. I'm good with power tools. I know how to use a pressure hose —"

Mr. Yao cut him off and told him flat out he wasn't interested.

"The answer is no," Mr. Yao said.

"But, Mr. Yao, you didn't even let him finish!" I interjected.

"I don't need to let him finish. There's nothing handy about Hank, only *ma fan.* . . ." Mr. Yao said, and hung up.

I avoided Hank's gaze as I walked back into the front office.

"What's *ma fan* mean?" he asked.

"I don't know," I lied. I couldn't bring

myself to say that *ma fan* in Chinese meant "trouble."

Chapter 27

In school the next day, Mrs. Douglas gave us back our stories. I stared at mine, lying upside down on my desk.

"Please read my comments," Mrs. Douglas said. "I took a lot of time writing them. I've also graded your stories."

A hand shot up.

"Did anyone get an A?"

"Yes, of course," Mrs. Douglas said.

"Well, did anyone get a C?"

"Stop fishing, Dillon," Mrs. Douglas said.

All around me, my classmates started turning their stories around. I looked over at Lupe and watched as she turned hers over and a small smile escaped on her lips.

I looked down at my own story. With a deep breath, I turned it around.

There, plastered in red ink, on the very top of my essay was a big, fat C-minus.

Twelve. That's the number of exclamation

marks my teacher used to describe how bad my writing was.

Check your grammar!!!! Tenses, Mia, don't forget tenses!!!! You NEED to proofread!!!!

The little minus sign on the top of the page winked at me, reminding me that C wasn't bad enough, it had to be C-minus. I stared at the red marks all over my story, a hot, bloody mess. In every sentence, there was something circled or crossed out. *Why couldn't I ever get the tenses right?*

I could hear my mom's voice in my head shouting, *Because there are no tenses in Chinese!* My mother was right. How could I possibly be as good as the other kids in their language? I should just forget about the essay contest. Who was I kidding? I didn't stand a chance. If I entered, it would just be $300 down the toilet.

I stared at my classmates, drinking in their glee as they proudly waved their stories around. I couldn't stop looking at them, showing off their grades, grinning from ear to ear. I envied them with every bone in my body.

When at last the school bell rang, I skulked home, my legs like Jell-O, my feet cement blocks. The words *You are never getting off your roller coaster* played in my head like a news ticker.

■ ■ ■ ■

I stashed my C-minus story deep in my closet when I got home, along with the essay contest printout I had been saving. I thought if I hid it, I wouldn't have to ever think about it again, but that afternoon, the cable was acting up again and Lupe came over.

"So, what'd you get on your story?" Lupe asked.

I shook my head at her.

"You don't want to know," I mumbled. She shrugged.

"Oh, c'mon, it can't be that bad," she said. I didn't say anything.

"Who cares? It's just a grade," Lupe said. "You should have seen my grades when I first started going to school here."

But it wasn't just a grade! It meant I was no good at writing, and how was I supposed to win a motel if I wasn't any good at writing? Before I could help it, everything came pouring out.

Lupe's eyes bulged when she heard about the essay contest. For a second, I worried I had made a terrible mistake telling her. What if *she* applied for it herself?

But then she reached over, took one of

the guest comment cards, and scribbled something down. She handed me the card.

I looked down at it.

It said,

You can't win if you don't play.

I looked back up at Lupe.

"But it costs three hundred dollars to play!" I reminded her.

Lupe shrugged.

"My dad says in America you gotta pay to play," she said.

I looked out the window at her dad up on the roof, climbing down with all those thick wires around his shoulder.

Suddenly, Lupe got quiet.

"What's wrong?" I asked her.

"Nothing," she said.

I knew it wasn't nothing, so I asked her again.

"I'll be sad if you move away to Vermont," she whispered.

This almost knocked me over. It hadn't even *occurred* to me how she might feel if I won. She had to know that there was no chance I'd win.

"I just got a C-minus, remember?"

I thought this would make her laugh, but it didn't. Lupe just kept staring at the floor.

She didn't even look up when her dad came in and told her it was time to go.

"See ya tomorrow," I said.

"See ya," Lupe muttered.

As she pushed open the front office door, she turned and said, "Oh, and, Mia?"

"Yes?"

"I hope you win."

Her words warmed me to my toes.

CHAPTER 28

When you've moved schools as many times as I have, you start to think of everyone as temporary. Friends come and go. You might have a best friend, but you know in the back of your mind, she's not always going to be there. You'll change schools or she'll change schools, and that'll be that.

For years, I told myself that was okay. That was just the way it was, kind of like replacing a toothbrush. Sure, you might like your toothbrush a lot. But sooner or later, you'd have to replace it. You'd get a new toothbrush, and it might feel strange and uncomfortable at first, but then you'd get used to it.

I guess I never thought about how the toothbrush might feel.

I never thought the toothbrush would miss me.

I was walking through the motel, still thinking about Lupe, when my dad waved me over to room 8.

"Look what a customer left on the table!"

I stepped into the room and saw a five-dollar bill and three one-dollar bills lying on the table along with a note:

To the little girl who checked us in,
keep doing a great job!

"Eight dollars!" my dad exclaimed. "You know what that means!"

I smiled.

Chinese people believe that if you receive eight dollars, it's good luck. That's because the word for the number eight, ba, rhymes with the word for "prosperity," fa.

It was such a nice surprise that I went back to the front office to write the customers a thank-you note. As I got their registration card out and copied down their address, it briefly crossed my mind that maybe I should stop. Given the grade I'd just gotten in English, did I really know what I was doing?

But then I thought about Lupe, and how she said you can't win if you don't play. I now had eight more dollars to play with, eight dollars that had just dropped down from the sky. I *had* to say thank you.

I went over to Mrs. T's room to try and borrow a dictionary. Mrs. T was always reading. With her cat-eye glasses, she sat by the pool and plowed through at least two newspapers and a magazine a day. Not only did Mrs. T have a dictionary, but she was delighted to lend me hers. It was a massive book, almost as thick as the Yellow Pages.

It wasn't just a dictionary either; it had something called a thesaurus too. A thesaurus, Mrs. T said, was a list of words that meant the same thing as other words. You could trade them freely, like you can trade one US dollar for eight Chinese renminbi.

I carried Mrs. T's nifty dictionary-thesaurus over to the front office and started composing my letter.

Dear Mr. and Mrs. Miller,

Thank you so much for the $8 tip ~~alone~~ along with the ~~good~~ kind note. It ~~helped my day~~ made my day, and I was ~~have~~ having a bad day. I got a bad grade at school. It was so bad that I was ~~thought~~ thinking about ~~not doing~~ giving up ~~in~~ on something.

But then two things ~~happen~~ happened — my friend from school ~~says~~ said something nice to me and I ~~get~~ got your note and tip. I think that's a sign, ~~do you~~

don't you?

My parents ~~believe in~~ are big on signs. I'm not, especially if they are bad. But I like the good ones. ☺

Thanks for ~~give~~ giving me a good sign. And thanks for staying ~~in~~ at the Calivista. I hope you'll come again soon.

Sincerely,
Mia Tang
Assistant Manager

I worked with Mrs. T's thick dictionary-thesaurus, trading words, looking things up, learning phrases like "big on" and "made my day," crossing things out, and trying things on until at last, I was satisfied with my letter. I copied the letter over onto a clean sheet of paper, sealed the envelope, and placed it in the outgoing mail pile.

Then I had another idea. If Mr. and Mrs. Miller were willing to give me a tip, maybe other guests would be as well. Who knew? Maybe if I saved up, I could have enough to enter the essay contest. I called up Lupe.

"That's a great idea!" she said. "You should totally do it."

Lupe said everyone was always giving out tips in restaurants. Even her dad, if he did an extra good job, got a tip from his customers. Except Mr. Yao, of course. Mr. Yao never gave Lupe's dad a tip, not even on Christmas day last year when he had to go over to his house to repair the cable.

The tip jar would have to be a secret, though. Mr. Yao couldn't see it. If he saw it, he'd just take the money like he took everything else. I wasn't even sure I wanted my parents to see it. They still didn't know about the essay contest. If my mom knew, she might say I didn't stand a chance. And the last thing I needed was her telling me I couldn't do it.

I hung up the phone and went to the kitchen, where I found an empty plastic jar. I taped a Post-it on the front of it and wrote the words *Tip Jar.* I added some stars for good measure.

I put the jar on the front desk. I decided I would only put it out when it was just me. When my parents or Mr. Yao were around, or when I was at school, I'd hide it under the desk.

I lifted the divider and stood back to admire the jar. It looked good there.

I went out the back to return Mrs. T's dictionary back to her. As I was walking across the parking lot, I noticed a couple I'd just checked in going up to my mom, who was walking back from one of the rooms. They were holding a camera.

171

"Excuse me, will you take a picture of us?" the woman asked my mom. She grinned at her boyfriend. "This is our first vacation together."

"Your first vocation? That's great!" my mom said in her broken English.

"Vacation," the couple corrected. "Anyway, will you take our picture?"

"Sure!" my mom said, taking the camera from her.

The couple showed her which button to push, and I could tell my mom was tingling with excitement because she kept running her fingers along the zoom. Finally! A real camera!

As my mom put her eye to the viewfinder, the couple hugged each other and gave her great big toothy grins.

"Eggplant!" my mom said. Except she pronounced it "Eggplan'."

The woman frowned a little.

"You know, it's eggplant," said the woman after my mom put the camera down.

"What?"

"Eggplan*t*," the woman said, emphasizing the *t* so vigorously she was practically spitting on my mom.

I could feel the heat of my mom's embarrassment from where I was standing.

"If you're going to say it, you should say it

right. And really, you should be saying 'cheese,' " the woman said as she walked off with her camera.

My mom just stood there, looking so sad I wanted to run up to her and tell her, *Hey, it's okay. I just got a C-minus on my English story. I know how you feel.*

But I knew this would not make her feel better. It would only make her feel worse.

It almost made me want to do more math.

CHAPTER 29

Jason was back at school the next day. He hadn't been since the day in the auditorium. Mrs. Douglas still said it was because he was sick.

I felt bad and was kind of worried about him, but now seeing him in his seat, glaring at me and snickering with some of the other kids, I saw that he was perfectly all right. He just had a bad case of the I-Hate-Mias.

Slowly, I walked over to my desk and took a seat beside him. He and his friends stopped talking, but I could feel their eyeballs on me. I could feel them sinking into my pants.

I had on a pair of these thin, floral pants my mom got from Goodwill. I'll admit it, they looked a lot like pajama pants, but they were $6.99 for a bundle of six and you couldn't beat that.

"What a deal!" my mom had squealed in the store when she spotted them. "Your mom has the *best* shopping eyes."

She had seemed so proud and so happy, I let her buy them for me. And they *were* pretty comfortable. But now, as my eyes slid over to the other kids, all of them in jeans, I wondered if it was a horrible mistake.

I used to have jeans too. In fact, I boarded the plane in a brand-new pair of jeans that my aunt bought for me in Beijing. But they were too small on me now. And a new pair of jeans costs $9.99 — much too expensive considering how quickly I was growing. Since coming to the motel, I had grown a full inch, a fact not lost on Mr. Yao, who motioned with his greasy fingers every time he came over. "See that growth? I paid for that growth!"

"Hey, Mia," Jason said loudly.

I looked over at him.

He glanced at the other kids, who were all covering their mouths with their hands, like they were trying to hold in some terrific inside joke.

"How come you always wear those pants?" Jason asked.

The other kids exploded with laughter.

I shifted my body away from them. My pants, seconds ago so soft and comfortable, now felt scorching hot.

■ ■ ■ ■

"Ignore them," Lupe said.

We were sitting on the grass at recess. I glared at Jason and his friends, who were sitting on the other side, cracking up and pointing at me.

"He'll get bored and move on to someone else," Lupe said. Somehow, I doubted that, and not five seconds later, Jason yelled at us from across the playground.

"Has she not heard of jeans?" Jason hollered to thunderous laughter.

That's it. I couldn't take it anymore. I got up, only to be pulled back down by Lupe.

"*Ignore* them," she repeated. She was being very calm about the whole thing, annoyingly calm if you asked me.

If my cousin Shen were here, he'd be over there in two seconds. Back in China, if anybody picked on me at school, he would go up to them and give them a piece of his mind. He didn't care who it was, even if it was his best friend, a fidgety kid with glasses named Mo. Mo always liked to go up to me and pull on my ponytail, and one time, he pulled too hard and I cried. Shen told Mo if he ever did it again, he'd pull his ear down to his butt. Mo kept his fingers to himself after that.

I tried not to think about those memories. Instead, I tried to focus on the words Lupe was saying now. She was telling me about her grandmother in Mexico and how she was sick, so her mom was sending money home. That's why money was tight for their family. I nodded as I listened, trying hard not to look down. Because despite everything she was saying, Lupe was still wearing jeans.

CHAPTER 30

Mr. Yao was at the motel when I got home. Hank had stopped paying his rent. But he wasn't moving out — he had done some research and discovered a law in California that said that if someone lived somewhere continuously for more than thirty days, that made them a tenant. That gave them certain rights, including the right not to be kicked out all of a sudden, even if they stopped paying rent.

"Now you listen to me, Hank. You pay up right this minute!" Mr. Yao pounded on Hank's door.

I immediately threw the blue baseball cap onto the front desk, hid my tip jar in my room, and went out the back to join my parents. They were standing awkwardly next to Mr. Yao in front of Hank's. Mr. Yao had apparently insisted they come with him — he said it was for "training purposes."

Hank opened the door.

"Pay up or get out," Mr. Yao said, jabbing his finger at Hank. "It's as simple as that."

"Check your facts, Yao," Hank said. "I've been staying here for six months. That makes me a resident. You can't just kick out a resident like that," he finished, with a snap of his fingers.

Mr. Yao shook his head. "That can't be right. You've been here for *six months?*"

He turned to my parents.

"It's true," my parents said.

"How did we ever let this street-rat weasel his way in here?" Mr. Yao fumed.

"Well, this has been lovely," Hank said, closing the door in Mr. Yao's face.

Mr. Yao pounded on the door, shouting, "You're a loser" and "This isn't over!" When Hank refused to open up, Mr. Yao turned to my parents. "You two, in my office, NOW!"

My parents exchanged worried looks as they followed him back to the front office. For the next fifteen minutes, I listened to Mr. Yao yammer on and on at my parents from my room. He said that if Hank did not pay up, we would have to pay for Hank. He was going to take the rent straight out of our salary.

Anger brewed inside me, scalding hot.

CHAPTER 31

At school, Jason continued making fun of my clothes. Even the sixth graders were in on it now. At first, I managed to convince myself that it was kind of flattering that they were even talking about me, but then I heard what they said.

In the bathroom, a couple of sixth-grade girls were gossiping.

"Her pants! Oh my God, have you seen her pants?" they asked each other while I sat in the stall.

"It's like she buys her clothes by the pound."

"My *grandmother* dresses better than her!"

I sat on the toilet, waiting for them to leave, my heart clenching like a fist.

Dear mean girls,

~~Your~~ You're right. I ~~by~~ buy my clothes by the pound. My mom and I go over to the Goodwill and we buy ~~old~~ second-hand clothes. Clothes you probably ~~through~~ threw away. I'm probably wearing your socks right now.

Let me tell you what it's like to ~~by~~ buy second-hand clothes. First, my mom ~~washs~~ washes it a million times. She ~~scrub~~ scrubs it with her hands and then ~~put~~ puts it in the washer and then ~~scrub~~ scrubs it again. Still, when I first put it on, I wriggle and ~~squirms~~ squirm, thinking of all the girls who've been inside the pants before.

I used to hope it was girls like you. Girls who ~~lives~~ live in big houses. Girls who ~~goes~~ go on vacation in the summer. I used to think that ~~meybe~~ maybe if I was wearing the same pants, I kind of went on vacation ~~two~~ too. And that used to make me happy.

Now do you ~~no~~ know what I think? I think I'd rather never go on vacation ~~then~~ than be like you.

Mia Tang

P.S. Floral cotton pants are way more comfy ~~then~~ than jeans.

It was so satisfying writing the letter that, for a full second, I actually thought about putting it into my backpack and giving it to the girls at school. But I didn't.

School dragged on. The popular girls continued mocking me. Mr. Yao called up twice a day to scream at us. The only thing that made me feel a tiny bit better was that somebody left five dollars in the tip jar after their stay.

One afternoon, while I was sitting at the front desk, a beat-up old Chevrolet slowed by the motel. It inched toward us, the driver craning his neck as he peered in. I squinted inside the car and saw a Chinese man.

I figured he must be a friend of Aunt Ling's, looking for the blue baseball cap, so I immediately waved at him to come in. Mr. Yao wasn't here — the coast was clear!

Uncle Zhu was a big man, about six foot two.

"Two hundred pounds of Northern Chinese," he said proudly in his thick Harbin accent.

My dad pointed at his compact car. "And you've been sleeping in that thing?" Uncle Zhu had explained that he hadn't had a place to sleep for a little while.

"It's been a hard couple of weeks," he said, stretching as he said the words.

"Well, let's get you a proper shower and a meal," my dad said, leading him toward room 3.

At dinner, Uncle Zhu told us he had been working as a janitor in a hospice.

"What's a hospice?" I asked.

"It's . . ." He thought for a minute about how to put it. "It's basically a waiting room."

"You mean like at the airport?" I asked. The day I left China, Shen had pointed to the waiting room in the arrival section right before I got on the plane.

"I'll see you right there in a couple of years, okay?" he had said.

I nodded. Tears stung the backs of my eyes.

"The time will flash by like *wooom*," he'd said. Then he looked down at the floor and whispered, "And when you come back, you'll be all American."

"No, I won't!" I insisted.

"Will too."

"Nothing's going to change, Shen."

"Yes, it will," he said. "You're going to come back wearing all kinds of fancy clothes."

Oh, Shen, if you only knew.

I looked up from my floral pants to Uncle Zhu.

"So is that what it is? A waiting room for arrivals?" I asked.

He glanced at my parents, as if to get their

183

permission. They nodded at him.

"It's a waiting room . . . for people who are about to pass away," he finally said.

Oh.

Ever so quietly, my mother picked up the last of the beef with her chopsticks and set it down onto Uncle Zhu's plate.

Uncle Zhu set off for San Diego the next morning. When I heard San Diego, I dashed to the front office and jotted down another one of the addresses. Uncle Zhu promised he'd drive by and call me if he saw the Thunderbird.

As my dad and I waved to Uncle Zhu, suddenly, I had an idea. I turned to my dad.

"What if we hide Hank like the immigrants?" I asked him. "Then Mr. Yao would stop screaming at us. He would never know."

My dad shook his head and said that it was way too risky. The immigrants only stayed for one night, whereas Hank lived here. We were bound to get caught. I decided to drop it. A week later, my parents received their paycheck from Mr. Yao: $140 was missing. True to his word, Mr. Yao was making us pay for Hank, twenty dollars per day.

My parents got into a big fight about what

to do. My mother said we should quit, but my dad wouldn't hear of it.

"Quit?" my dad said. "And do what? You think it's any better out there? You heard the stories from all the immigrants!"

My mother didn't respond but instead went into the kitchen and pulled out stinky tofu paste from the back of the cupboard. Stinky tofu paste was this disgusting concoction you could buy at the Chinese supermarket, which she ate whenever she'd "been through a lot." And even though I didn't like the smell of the tofu, I still liked it more than hearing my parents fighting.

As my mom munched away on her paste, my dad and I sat outside by the curb, waiting for the smell to clear. The early evening wind sighed between us.

I wanted to tell him it was going to be okay. That I had a plan to save us. All I needed was $300 and I even had a plan for that too. So far, I had made thirty dollars in tips.

But I didn't end up telling him. I was worried if he knew about the thirty dollars, he might take it away. And then I wouldn't be able to save us.

CHAPTER 32

In school, the next day, Mrs. Douglas clapped her hands together and announced we were having a math challenge.

"No! No! We're not ready!" we insisted. But Mrs. Douglas wouldn't hear any of it. She split us into teams of four. We were to work together to solve one "extra-tough" math question, and the first team with the right answer was the winner. Jason, thankfully, was *not* on my team. But Bethany, Joanne, and Paula were, and they were three of the most popular girls in our year. I braced for more jokes about my pants.

To my surprise, when they heard I was on their team, they cheered.

"YES! We got the Chinese girl!"

I took a seat next to my new teammates and smiled. I gazed up at the board, pencil ready, determined not to let my team down.

I couldn't believe my eyes when Mrs. Douglas finished writing the problem on the board — it was a problem about a motel!

The daily rate for a room at a motel is thirty dollars a day. A customer at a motel wants to rent the room for just 2 hours. How much does the motel charge the customer?

I glanced at Jason, who looked similarly stoked. I clutched my pencil tighter. No way was I letting him win this.

"Thirty dollars!" I said to my teammates immediately. Just because someone leaves early, you don't give him a discount.

Bethany tossed her blond hair over her shoulder and looked hesitantly at me. "Are you sure?" she asked, "Shouldn't it be cheaper?"

I shook my head. *Trust me,* I wanted to say, *I've been doing this a long time.*

"It's thirty dollars," I repeated. "I'm positive."

My group went with my answer, raising their hands to tell Mrs. Douglas. But as soon as we told Mrs. Douglas our answer, she shook her head and said it was *wrong!*

"That is not the correct answer," she said.

Angry eyes turned to me.

"YOU said it was thirty dollars!" my teammates yelled at me.

"I . . . I'm sorry," I muttered.

"You're Chinese! You're *supposed* to be good at math!"

"She's not Chinese," Joanne said. Her eyes dropped to my pants. "She's ugly-nese."

The words sliced into me.

By the time we went back and started calculating 2/24 × $30, Jason's group already blurted out the correct answer — $2.50. We had lost the math challenge.

"Bravo!" Mrs. Douglas said, handing Jason's team cherry lollipops as she clapped her hands again and asked us to return to our original seats.

Jason sat next to me sucking loudly on his lollipop, boasting his victory with every lick.

"Guess it's official," he said, "I'm better than you at math!"

I wanted to remind him that I was there when his dad screamed at him for being terrible at math, or had he forgotten? But that would have been too Jason of me.

As Jason sucked away on his lollipop, I looked around at all the other kids. Lupe and everyone else were chatting and laughing even though they also lost, while Bethany, Joanne, and Paula continued glaring at me from across the room. I could feel their disappointment on my back, shoulders, everywhere.

I put my head down at my desk, wondering if I looked more like the other kids in

my class — if I had blond hair and blue eyes
— then would it be okay that I sucked at
math?

CHAPTER 33

I pulled my hair back. I was standing in front of the mirror in the manager's quarters, the afternoon traffic a dull rumbling in my ears.

I glanced over to the kitchen. There was a banana on the table. I stared at it, at its bold yellow hue.

I walked over and picked it up. My eyes searched the room — it was just me in the manager's quarters. Quickly, I peeled the banana and walked over to the mirror again. I held the banana peel up, higher and higher until it reached my head, then carefully draped the banana peel over my jet-black hair.

Hesitantly, I looked into the mirror. The "blond" me smiled back.

I stared and stared, so mesmerized by the reflection that I completely did not hear the back door opening and my mom coming in.

My mother shrieked when she saw me.

"What the heck are you doing?" she cried, pointing at the banana peel hugging my hair, the stem on top of my head.

I instantly wiped the smile off my face. I yanked the banana peel off my head and threw it into the trash.

"Why?" my mother demanded. "Why would you put a banana peel on your head?" She fished the peel out of the trash and placed it on the kitchen table. There it lay, limp and mushy, proof of my embarrassing little experiment.

"Well?" my mom asked, her arms folded.

"I . . . I was just trying something out," I said.

"What were you trying out?"

I said nothing.

"Did something happen at school today?" she asked.

I bit my lower lip. I could feel my chin quivering.

My mother's face softened.

"It's okay," she said. "You can tell me."

The tears came gushing out before the words did. I ran into my mother's arms. I told her how I got a math question wrong and the other kids mocked me, saying I should have gotten it right because I'm Chinese.

When my mother heard that, she removed

her arms. A new look took over her face —
a look I did not like at all.

"They're right," she said. I took a step
back, shaking my head. *No,* she's not really
saying that. She can't possibly be siding with
them.

She can and she was.

"How can you get a math problem wrong?
What were you thinking?"

My dad came in to see what all the com-
motion was about.

"What's going on?"

"Your daughter just got a math question
wrong at school, that's what's going on,"
she informed him. I was always "your
daughter" when she wasn't happy with me
and "my daughter" when she was.

I looked down at the floor. I heard my dad
offer, "It's okay. . . ." To which my mother
snapped, "No, it's *not* okay!"

She walked over, put her cold hands on
my hot cheeks, and yelled, "Math's all
you've got!"

That did it.

"I don't even like math!" I screamed back
at her. "I like English!"

My mother's eyes widened.

"English?" she exclaimed.

I nodded. My heart thudded in my chest.
One second passed. And then another. And

then, softly, my mother breathed out a tornado.

"You know what you are in English? You're a bicycle, and the other kids are cars."

CHAPTER 34

That night, I sat at the stairwell in the back thinking of something my uncle once said. He said that if you break a bowl, you can put all the pieces back together, but it will never be the same. Water will seep through the cracks. That's what it felt like when my mom called me a bike — like our bowl shattered and we'd never be whole again.

Mrs. Q spotted me sitting on the stairwell and came over and sat down next to me. She asked me what was wrong. I shook my head. I didn't know how to tell her the worries swirling in my head:

1. My mom was horrible and mean.
2. She hated me.
3. What she said was true.

At the thought of number three, the tears welled in my eyes again. Mrs. Q pulled me into her arms. Between sobs, she got it out of me what happened.

"Oh, honey," she said, rubbing my back. "Sometimes adults say stupid things they don't mean."

I rubbed my nose. "But she does mean it! She totally means it!"

I thought of all the times my mom had said my English was not as good as the white kids', and I cried even harder. My tears stained Mrs. Q's lovely new shirt, and Mrs. Q glanced down at the wet spot.

"I'm sorry!" I said.

"It's okay," she said, smoothing out her shirt. "Nothing that can't be fixed with a good wash."

She smiled at me. "Just like you and your mom."

"No way," I said, shaking my head. I looked at Mrs. Q with utmost resolve. "The bowl is broken. There's no unbreaking it."

"Easy now," Mrs. Q said. She put her hand over my hand. "I don't know about any bowls, but I do know your mom. And she loves you very much."

There was a lump in my throat.

Mrs. Q raised her soft blue eyes to my wet brown ones.

"You know that, don't you?" she asked.

"Then why is she always saying such mean things?" I asked.

Mrs. Q thought about this for a while.

"I don't know," she finally said. "Your mom's been working a lot lately. She's probably tired. Stressed out. Heck, maybe this isn't even about you. Maybe this is about her. Maybe people have told her *her* English isn't good. . . ."

I thought about that couple a while back who asked my mom to take a picture of them with their camera.

"Still doesn't make it okay what she said," I said, sniffling.

"Of course not," she said.

"It's a horrible thing to say."

"Of course it is."

"Even if the bowl's completely not broken, it's *severely* cracked," I told her. Mrs. Q chuckled.

"Well, you'll just have to put some tape around it," she said.

A tiny smile escaped.

I hugged Mrs. Q and thanked her. I was starting to feel a little bit better about number one and number two on my list. But not number three. Number three I carried with me into my sleep, dreaming about the essay contest and how I could possibly win if I was only a bike.

That Sunday, my dad fought my mother for

the chance to take me out. As usual, we loaded up the car with empty cans. We went to the recycling center, then after that, instead of exchanging for pennies and going to the lake, my dad made an unexpected turn. Into a shopping center.

My dad *hates* shopping. What was going on?

"Where are we going?" I asked him.

"You'll see," he said, getting out of the car.

He pressed open the door of a stationery shop. The store was called Scribbles and I could tell it was fancy just from the way it smelled. It smelled like expensive air freshener, the kind I always wanted to get for our front office but couldn't because it was way too expensive. Row upon row of pencils adorned the shelves. I picked one of them up and nearly fainted when I saw the price. *$5.99!*

I tugged on my dad's elbow.

"Let's go home," I said.

"Just a second," he said. Before I could even realize what was happening, he took one of the $5.99 pencils and told the cashier to ring it up.

"Dad, what are you doing?" I asked him.

He ignored me and handed the cashier six dollars — the entirety of our recycling money that day. I watched the whole thing unfold with my mouth open. Outside the shop, my dad kneeled down so that he was my level.

"You are not a bicycle," he said.

My eyes searched his.

"Do you understand?" he asked.

He reached down, took my small hand, and opened it. He put the new, expensive pencil in it.

I gazed down at the pencil. Its shiny green sparkles glistened in the light. I couldn't believe my eyes that something so beautiful could sit in my hands.

"Dad, this is . . . this is way too nice . . ." I said, giving him a hug. "I'm never even going to use it — I'm just going to look at it!"

My dad laughed. "Oh, I hope you use it. You're a fine story writer," he said.

I shook my head.

"Not in English . . ." I said in a small voice.

"In English too," he insisted. "I've read your English."

I wanted to chuckle because how would he know? If my English was twelve-exclamation-marks bad, his had to be at least fifty! Still, his words made me feel warm and toasty, and I tucked them into my pocket.

"Use this to write down everything that happens," he said. "Who knows, maybe someday, it'll all seem funny to you."

Maybe.

I nodded and smiled, holding my brand-new pencil up to the sun.

CHAPTER 35

When we got back to the motel, there was another Chinese immigrant waiting for us. Word was really getting out about the baseball cap!

Uncle Fung was an animated guy with thick eyebrows that moved up and down as he talked. He told us that he used to be an accountant back in China and now was working as a waiter over in Riverside. That was, until he got fired.

"You won't believe this boss of mine," he said at dinner. This time, my mom made lettuce. Literally, just lettuce. Thanks to Mr. Yao withholding our wages, it was all we could afford. But stir fried with a little garlic and soy sauce, it actually wasn't half bad.

"What'd he do?"

"He fired me for scratching my nose!"

"What?" I said. "Really?"

"That and the fact that a customer slapped me, which by the way was completely uncalled for."

"A customer *slapped* you?" my mom asked.

"She was crazy! I honestly don't know why she slapped me," he said. "All I said to her was 'Hey, baby.' "

My mom nearly choked on her tea.

"Well, no wonder she slapped you!" my dad said.

Uncle Fung put his chopsticks down.

"What's wrong with 'Hey, baby'? Americans are always saying 'Hey, baby.' It's what you say when you greet somebody — everybody knows that." He shrugged.

"It's what you say when you greet a girlfriend or boyfriend," my mom told him.

Uncle Fung turned bright red. "Are you serious?" he asked.

My mom nodded. Uncle Fung got up and started pacing the room. He put his hands to his face.

"I had no idea!" he said. "So many people were saying it, I just thought . . ."

My dad chuckled.

"It's all right, buddy. Happens to the best of us," he said.

"I *cannot* believe this. I was saying it to almost everyone," Uncle Fung said, scratching his nose.

Something about the way he was scratching his nose caught my eye. He was scratching with his middle finger!

"Um . . . Uncle Fung?" I asked.

"Yeah?" he said.

He turned to me, his middle finger still on his nose. From a distance, it looked like he was flipping me off.

"What? What is it?"

He looked so innocent and earnest and at the same time so ridiculous, I just had to help him.

That night, I made Uncle Fung a pamphlet of American phrases and what they actually meant.

Mia's Book of American Phrases and Customs:

— When you hear "get out of here," do not actually get out of there. It's just something people say when they're surprised.

— If someone says something is a "piece of cake," it doesn't mean they're going to give you cake. It just means it's easy.

— Do not be alarmed when you hear the phrase "riding shotgun." It doesn't mean they have a gun. It means to sit next to the driver in the car.

— Don't feel insulted when you hear the

202

word "dawg" as in "What's up, dawg?" or "How you doing, dawg?" Dawg means "friend." If someone is calling you a "dawg," they are not being rude and calling you a "dog."

— If something is sweet, like "Sweet car!" it means it is good. It does not mean it literally tastes sweet.

— Similarly, if something is "sick," as in "Sick bike!" it also means good. I know it's a little confusing.

— The word "dude" is a slang term for a male friend. It should not be used when addressing the police, your boss, a senior citizen, or a female.

— Do not stick your middle finger up for any reason in America because the middle finger is considered offensive. Use your index finger or pinkie instead to scratch your face.

— Don't take your shoes off everywhere. Americans like to wear their shoes inside the house.

— Do not comment on how someone's appearance has changed. I know it's a compliment in China to say, "You look like you've gained weight!" but trust me, Americans do not like it.

The pamphlet went on and on. I tried to

be as detailed as possible and put in as many phrases, gestures, and idioms as I could think of.

Uncle Fung was very grateful when I gave him the pamphlet. He said he would study it and memorize the rules before he applied for his next job. I also showed him my notebook with all the names of the restaurants the other immigrants had gotten fired from so he knew where to avoid working.

Uncle Fung copied the restaurants down and added some names of his own. He also added some comments next to the others' stories, such as "Hang in there" and "I feel your pain, brother." I smiled. I liked how my little notebook was becoming a message board for the immigrants.

Uncle Fung left the next day as the first of many jack-o'-lanterns appeared in Mrs. Q's window. It was almost Halloween, and I hadn't really thought anything of it. But then I started making a killing in tips! I guess people felt sorry for me, because every single customer who came through on Halloween put five dollars in my jar. They probably thought I should be out trick-or-treating instead of working in a motel.

You know who else thought I should be out trick-or-treating? The weeklies.

"It's Halloween!" Mrs. Q said. "You gotta go trick-or-treating on Halloween if you're a kid. You just *gotta*!"

"I don't have a costume," I said with a shrug.

"No costume, huh?" Mrs. Q asked. "Be right back."

An hour later, Mrs. Q came back all wrapped up in toilet paper. So were all the other weeklies! They were mummies!

"Trick or treat!" the weeklies announced.

My face brightened when I saw Hank. It'd been a while since I saw a smile on his face.

"C'mon, Mia," Hank said, handing me a roll of toilet paper. "Let's go get you some candy."

I took the toilet paper and hopped off the stool just as my parents came into the front office.

"You might want to wait ten minutes," my mom said.

"Why?" I asked.

"I hear our cable's down," she said with a wink.

A small smile escaped from my lips. Though I was still mad at my mom for calling me a bike, I thought it was very cool that she had called Lupe.

Lupe, the weeklies, and I walked up and

down Meadow Lane under the moonlit sky, all of us dressed up as mummies. Lupe and I giggled under the toilet paper, going up and pressing on doorbells. As we walked, I asked Lupe whether there was Halloween in Mexico. Lupe said there was something similar called Day of the Dead, when people would pay their respects to deceased loved ones by visiting cemeteries and building altars called ofrendas. At the mention of deceased loved ones, Lupe got really quiet. I guess she was thinking about her grand-mother.

"Are you going to go back and visit your grandmother?" I asked her.

Mexico was so close, just a few hours away by car.

Lupe shook her head. "I don't know," she said. She didn't seem to want to talk about it.

"What about you?" Mrs. T asked me. "You guys have Halloween in China?"

I laughed. "No way," I said.

I told Lupe and the weeklies about our first Halloween in America, how we didn't know what it was and were so freaked out by strangers coming up to our door dressed as goblins and witches that we turned all the lights out and hid behind our sofa. Lupe laughed so hard bits of Reese's Peanut Butter Cup came flying out of her mouth.

I smiled.

In total that evening, we got eighteen candy bars, five Reese's Peanut Butter Cups, twenty-seven Tootsie Rolls, five packets of Skittles, and six Lemonheads.

Hank said we did well. He explained that when it came to candy, there were multiple tiers — at the Top Tier, you have your full-sized candy bars, followed by your mints (Junior Mints, Peppermint Patties, etc.), and, all the way down at the Bottom Tier, lollipops and that sort of thing.

"You know what you guys are?" I asked the weeklies and Lupe.

"What?"

"Top Tier friends," I said.

Hand in hand, we walked back to the motel.

CHAPTER 36

The next Sunday, it was my mom's turn to take me out. I looked down at the shopping bags in her hand.

My mom's favorite thing to do besides math was go shopping. Well, not shopping exactly. We walked around the mall with empty shopping bags filled with toilet paper.

We'd found the empty shopping bags in the mall parking lot a while back. There was a bright red one from Macy's and one from Mervyn's and a shimmery, silvery one from this store called Charlotte Russe. My mother was so happy when we found them. She immediately went into the mall bathroom and stuffed them with toilet paper. Now, every time we went to the mall, we carried them. My mom says that people are nicer to you if you walk around with a shopping bag.

As usual, we poked around Macy's. A sales lady came up to us and asked if we needed any help. My mom said her line: "I'm just looking." Usually, just being around new clothes cheered her up. Today, though, she seemed extra sad.

"I don't know what we're going to do," she said. "The extra twenty dollars a day for Hank is killing us, just killing us."

She shook her head.

"Maybe I could take a part-time job," she said. "I could see if any of the restaurants —"

"A part-time job? But what about Dad?" I protested. Dad had enough trouble as it was, even with her help. He got so little sleep from being up all night, checking customers in. Some days, he didn't even eat dinner after he finished cleaning. He just crashed onto the bed in the living room.

"Well, I have to do something," my mother said.

Once again, I thought about my tips. I had about a hundred dollars now. I was hiding it under my bed in a ziplock bag.

My mother poked me.

"Hey, isn't that . . . ?" she asked, pointing. I looked up and saw Jason standing there with someone who must have been his mom — they looked exactly alike — seeming just as surprised to see us there.

Jason and his mother waved and walked

over to us. It was hard not to stare at Jason's mom, specifically the humongous diamond on her hand. I thought I might go blind.

"It's so good to finally meet you," Jason's mother said, extending a hand to my mother. "My husband's told me so much about you."

She glanced at my mother's shopping bags and arched an eyebrow.

"I didn't know you guys shopped here," she said. My mother's face turned the same color as her shopping bag.

"We're just looking," she muttered. While she and my mother talked, Jason turned to me.

"Are you buying new pants?" he hissed.

"Are you buying a new face?" I hissed back.

Jason tugged on his mom's arm. "Let's go," he said.

"We ought to get going," Mrs. Yao said.

"We should get back too," my mom said.

"It was so nice meeting you," Mrs. Yao said, fake-smiling at my mom. "We should get together sometime."

"Well, you have my number," my mom joked. Mrs. Yao laughed.

As we walked out of the store, I turned around and stuck my tongue out at Jason, who stuck his tongue out right back.

Once we were in our car, my mom started having a panic attack.

"Oh God, I knew we shouldn't have come. I had this feeling all day that something bad was going to happen, but I just ignored it," my mom cried, rocking herself back and forth in the driver's seat.

"Is this about bumping into Jason and his mom?" I asked her.

She stared at me with this manic look in her eyes.

"We didn't just bump into them. We bumped into them at *Macy's!*" she cried.

"So?"

"So don't you understand? People like us don't go to Macy's. Especially if we're paying twenty dollars a day for Hank. They're probably thinking we must have savings, and now they're going to try to squeeze us for even more money. Oh God, oh God!"

My mother opened her door and got out, gasping for air. I scrambled after her.

"This was all my fault," she said, shaking her head as she opened up the trunk. "I should have never kept those bags!"

Before I could stop her, she took them out and ripped them into shreds, right there in the parking lot.

We both stared at the tiny pieces of butchered paper. I thought about the day my mom found those bags, how she ran her hands over them and couldn't stop smiling all day. How sometimes, in the late afternoons, after she'd spent the entire day on her knees, scrubbing floor after floor after floor, she'd get the shopping bags out and just look at them. She didn't think I saw her.

But I did.

Things must be really bad for my mom to want to give all that up.

Once again, I thought about the hundred dollars hiding under my mattress. The guilt burned in my chest.

CHAPTER 37

I told Lupe the next day about bumping into Jason's mom at the mall.

"So what'd you do?" she asked.

"Nothing. We just left," I said.

She looked surprised.

"You think we'd *hang out* with her?" I asked.

"I don't know." She shrugged. "Maybe you guys went shopping together. Aren't you guys always trying to find a good deal?"

I hated it when she lumped me and Jason together.

"It's not 'guys.' It's 'guy.' Singular," I told her. "I like a good deal, sure. But I don't screw people over."

Lupe looked at the ground and didn't say anything. I started to feel bad. But I didn't apologize. I needed her to know Jason and I were not the same.

In class, we had wrapped up our China unit, thank God, and moved on to other countries in Asia.

"Who can tell me another place where a lot of things are manufactured, besides Asia?" Mrs. Douglas asked.

A hand shot up.

"Canada?" someone from the front row asked.

"Mexico!" Mrs. Douglas announced, ending the guessing pretty quickly.

I glanced over at Lupe, who looked like she wanted to crawl under her desk.

"Many of the factories there are called maquiladoras, and they make things for cheap," Mrs. Douglas explained.

"How cheap?" another kid asked.

"Very cheap," Mrs. Douglas said. She told us that at some maquiladoras, workers made as little as fifty cents an hour. This struck me as hugely unfair, and I immediately raised my hand.

"How can they pay their workers so little?" I asked Mrs. Douglas.

"It's supply and demand. Anytime a lot of people want a job and there aren't that many jobs, the salary goes down," Mrs. Douglas said.

I thought about Mr. Yao's comment when we first came, about how ten thousand other immigrants would take our job in two seconds if we quit.

"Okay, kids," Mrs. Douglas announced. "We're going to play a little game. It's called Hot Seat."

That got my classmates' attention. They all sat up straighter in their seats, only to slump back down seconds later when they realized Hot Seat was an *educational* game, not a game game. Here's the way Hot Seat worked:

- Mrs. Douglas picked someone at random to represent the maquiladoras.
- That person had ten minutes to prepare his or her opening statement.
- Then they had to sit in the Hot Seat and answer tough questions from the floor. The rest of the class was the floor.

"The harder the question, the better," Mrs. Douglas said.

With that, she reached into her hat of names and pulled out a piece of paper.

"Jason Yao!" she announced.

Jason groaned. Slowly, he pulled out his pencil and started writing out his statement while I sat next to him, jaw locked, eyebrows furrowed.

He was going DOWN.

"Good morning. My name is Jason Yao, and

I represent the maquiladoras of Mexi—"

My hand shot up in the air.

"Hey!" Jason protested. "I'm not even done reading my statement yet."

"Fine," I said. I put my hand down and waited with bated breath for him to finish.

Jason droned on about how big his factories were and how many T-shirts and umbrella stands they made every year. As soon as he finished, my hand shot back up.

"How does it feel to squeeze your workers for every last cent they have?" I asked.

"I don't . . . *squeeze* anyone," Jason said.

"You pay your workers fifty cents an hour. I'd call that squeezing," I said. I glanced at Mrs. Douglas, who gave me the thumbs-up sign to keep going.

"They don't *have* to work for me. Nobody's forcing them to," Jason said with a shrug.

"But they don't have a choice. They have to feed their family," I said.

"Well, that's their problem!" Jason said.

My classmates' heads bounced from Jason to me like it was a tennis match.

"What if you were in their position?" I asked Jason.

"If I were in their position, I'd appreciate having a job," he said. He looked hard at me. "Wouldn't you?"

My cheeks burned. I glanced over at Lupe. As usual, her mouth was clamped shut.

I turned back to Jason.

"You need them just as much as they need you," I said. "Without them, you wouldn't have a factory."

"Yeah. So?"

"So why don't you pay them more?" I yelled. "Why do you always have to take from them? Take, take, take, take!"

Every time I said "take," I lunged forward in my seat. The other kids joined in and soon everyone was chanting, "Take! Take! Take! Take! Take!"

"It's not my fault!" Jason shrieked. "It's supply and demand! Mrs. Douglas — help!"

Mrs. Douglas stepped in and took over, freeing Jason from the Hot Seat.

As Jason crawled back to his desk, Mrs. Douglas turned to me and said, "Boy that was really something. Well done, Mia! I had no idea you were so passionate about maquiladoras!"

I didn't either.

I caught up to Lupe after school.

"Hey, how come you didn't help me back there?" I asked her. Lupe shrugged.

"Didn't look like you needed my help,"

she said. She turned and started walking home.

I felt the sting of rejection. What was *up* with her? I wondered if it had anything to do with what I said earlier, when I chewed her out for lumping me and Jason in the same category. Had I gone too far?

I kicked the rocks on the side of the road and decided to take the long way home. About halfway back I wandered into a shopping plaza, where there was a Pizza Hut calling to me at the end of the buildings. I stopped and peered in.

Usually, just looking into a restaurant filled me up. All those smiley people, families sitting down for a delicious meal together. We didn't get to eat out much in China, because family meals were usually at my grandmother's house, but the few times we did go out, it was pretty funny. In China, people do not split the bill. It's considered very rude to do so or to not pay for a friend. As a result, people routinely got into fistfights in restaurants as customers pushed and shoved one another for the bill.

As a kid, I remember it being hilarious to sit there and watch grown people fighting. Sometimes the fighting got so bad, the waiters and waitresses would have to squeeze in and break it up. Sometimes it would take a whole pack of waitresses just to pin down one person.

There was absolutely none of that going on at Pizza Hut that day. Everybody was very civil. There was no shouting and no fighting — people were splitting the bill right down the middle.

I guess that's because in America, it's to each his own. Maybe that was why Lupe didn't stand up for me. Maybe it had nothing to do with what I said about me and Jason.

CHAPTER 38

Jason glared at me the next day. I could feel his anger vibrating off of him. I put my head down on my desk to avoid having to look at him, but when I looked up again, I noticed he was twirling a pencil. He was always doing this, but then I noticed it wasn't just any ordinary pencil this time.

It was *my* pencil, the one my dad got me!

"Hey, give me that!" I said, nearly jumping out of my chair. But Jason quickly held the sparkly green pencil beyond my reach.

I waved my hand frantically so that Mrs. Douglas could see what an emergency this was.

"Yes, Mia?" Mrs. Douglas said.

"Jason stole my pencil!" I said, narrowing my eyes at him. The words shot out of my mouth, sizzling hot.

Mrs. Douglas turned to Jason. "Is that true?"

Jason, expert faker that he was, feigned

shock and outrage. "Of course not! Mrs. Douglas, this is *my* pencil. I would never take anything from Mia!"

"Liar!" I exclaimed.

"That's enough, Mia," Mrs. Douglas said. "Both of you, up here now." She motioned with her finger for the two of us to come up to her desk.

I stared at my sparkly pencil in Jason's hand, which he clutched tightly with his sticky, sweaty fingers as we walked over to Mrs. Douglas.

"Is this about what happened at Hot Seat?" Mrs. Douglas asked.

"No!" Jason blurted at the same time I said, "Of course it is!"

"He's mad I won," I told Mrs. Douglas. "So he had to take the one thing . . . the one thing . . ."

Tears slammed into the back of my eyes as I tried to get the words out.

"You didn't win. There is no *winning* in Hot Seat. There's only sitting," Jason said.

"Give me the pencil," Mrs. Douglas said.

Jason handed it to her. I watched as she turned it 360 degrees.

"Hmmm . . . I don't see any name on it," Mrs. Douglas said.

"That's because it costs *five ninety-nine,*" I told her. That wasn't a pencil — that was practically jewelry. You can't just write your name on a piece of jewelry!

"Exactly. Which is why it *has* to be mine." Jason pointed at me. "You really think *she* can afford something this nice?"

My jaw dropped. What a thing to say!

"I'm afraid, without a name on it, we can't tell for sure whose it is," Mrs. Douglas said. I sucked in my breath, preparing for the worst — Mrs. Douglas was going to keep the pencil for herself. I should have known. She'd probably had her eye on it for days!

"There's only one thing to do," Mrs. Douglas said. "Break the pencil in half."

I gasped. How could she suggest such a thing? But before I could say anything, Jason shouted, "No! Don't break the pencil in half! Let her have it."

Mrs. Douglas smiled.

"Now we know who the true owner of the pencil is," she said. I held out a trembling hand.

"Jason," she decided.

Mrs. Douglas said that because I took so long responding to the proposal of breaking the pencil in half, I could not possibly be the rightful owner. And Jason, with his touching, heartfelt plea on behalf of the pencil, *must* be the rightful owner. So the pencil was his.

It was the stupidest, most unfair thing I'd ever heard, and I had to bite the inside of my cheeks to keep from crying.

On the way back to our desks, I turned to Jason and asked in a very small voice, "Please, Jason, can you give me my pencil back? It's very important to me."

He thought for a second. "It's important to you, huh?" he asked. I nodded.

Jason held my pencil up as if to give it to me, and I reached my hand out to take it. Then he whipped the pencil back, stuck out his tongue, and licked it. He licked my beautiful sparkly pencil up and down with his nasty, evil tongue.

I was so startled, I made a noise that came out as a half snort and half chirp, which only made him laugh. He stuck the pencil in his pocket right as the bell rang.

School was over, and Jason walked off with the nicest thing I had.

CHAPTER 39

Dear Jason,

~~I hate you.~~ Please give me back my pencil ~~OR ELSE I'M GOING TO PUNCH YOU IN THE FACE!~~ for the following reasons.

1. It's mine.

2. You have so many pencils including two really cool bendable ones you don't even use. ~~It's totally unfair.~~

3. That pencil cost a lot of money, and I know you saw us at Macy's but we were ~~just pretending~~ just looking. We do not have savings.

~~4. That pencil is really important to me. You have no idea how much it means to me.~~

Sincerely,
Mia

I crossed out number four because I knew he wouldn't care. If anything, it would only make him want to keep the pencil even more, just to irritate me. Wasn't that what this was all about?

The phone started ringing, and I put my pencil down. It was Mr. Yao. I frowned. Now what?

"Tell your parents I'm going to be gone this weekend," he said. I half listened as he explained how he was taking his family to Las Vegas. I was in no mood to listen to his vacation plans.

"What are you telling me this for?" I said into the phone.

"I'm *telling* you because you guys keep having all those issues with the cable," he said. "If you have any while I'm gone, I left José's number with my housekeeper."

I sat up in my stool.

"So you're not going to be at your house this weekend?"

"That's right."

"None of you? Not even Jason?"

"Right."

It occurred to me that there could be an opportunity here.

Lupe was less than enthused when I told her my plan.

"I don't know . . ." she said.

"What do you mean? All we have to do is

go over to his house after school and tell the housekeeper that we're from the Girl Scouts and we're here to sell cookies. Then we'll ask her if we can use the bathroom, and when you're using the bathroom, I'll sneak into Jason's room and get my pencil back!"

I had been over the plan with her three times already. It was perfect.

Lupe looked away.

"I don't want to get in trouble," she said.

"You're not going to get in trouble," I said. "They're *out of town*. It'll just be their housekeeper, if there's anyone even there. The whole thing's only going to take five minutes!"

Lupe shook her head. I crossed my arms. I was beginning to get really tired of this.

"You know you always do this," I said to her.

"Do what?"

"Chicken out."

"What do you mean?" she asked.

The fact that she didn't even know what I was talking about was even more infuriating.

"You never stand up for me!" I said to her. "I thought you were my friend!"

"You don't get it, do you?"

"Get what?"

226

"Nothing! Forget it!"

There was no mistaking it, the anger in her eyes.

"What are you talking about?" I asked her.

"I'm talking about you. *You're* going to Vermont! You can say all this crazy stuff to Jason because he likes you," she exclaimed. "What about me?"

I blinked in confusion.

"I can't go with you to Mr. Yao's house," she said. "My dad still needs Mr. Yao." Lupe squeezed her eyes shut. "Unlike you, we don't have another plan."

CHAPTER 40

The storm in Lupe's face stuck with me after she left.

I felt sick with regret, making her feel this way. After all she'd done for me. Lupe was my best friend — she was the one who told me about the roller coaster in the first place. If it wasn't for her, I wouldn't even know about it. And there I was, going on and on about my plan to get off of it without even thinking about her.

It should be *her* entering the contest, not me. Let's face it: She had a much better chance at winning anyway. I decided to write her a letter.

Dear Lupe,
I'm sorry I said all those things. I completely ~~understood~~ understand if you don't want to go to Mr. Yao's house with me. Actually, I've been thinking about it and I don't think I'm going to

go ~~neither~~ either. You're right. It's ~~two~~ too risky. We have to be careful. I might have a plan, but for now, we still ~~works~~ work for him. And as you say, we still need him.

About the plan — I've been thinking. Why don't you enter the essay contest? I can tell you what to write about. You probably have a better ~~shoot~~ shot at winning it (your grammar's a LOT better ~~then~~ than mine). If you win, maybe we can run it together. What do you think?

Your friend,
Mia

The next school day, I went very early to school to put the letter on Lupe's desk. I also had something special for Jason — but it wasn't the letter I wrote him. It was something else I had picked up recently from another Chinese immigrant.

When I was helping this uncle with his luggage, I had pulled too hard and got a blister on my hand. The man said he had just the thing, and gave me a little vial of Chinese medicine. It felt minty and cool on my finger, but when I reached up to tuck my bangs behind my ear, my minty finger got a little too close to my eye. I was crying in seconds.

So after I set Lupe's letter down on her desk, I practically soaked Jason's pencils with the same stuff that had made me cry. *Let's see him twirl these suckers now!*

Jason did not notice the gleam on his pencils when he sat down later that morning. He was too busy bragging about Las Vegas and all the great food he ate and the luxurious suite they stayed in.

"They had a pool with three pool slides! There was even a restaurant right smack in the —"

"When are you going to give me my pencil back?" I asked. I wanted to cut to the chase. I couldn't care less about his fancy pools, considering I stared at one all day.

"You mean *my* pencil?" He shrugged. "I gave it to my dog, Wealthy. It's probably all chewed up by now."

He *would* give it to his dog. And he *would* have a dog named Wealthy.

Jason smirked, picked up one of his pencils and started twirling. He twirled it a little too close to his face and just as I predicted, the strong minty smell made his eyes water. He put the pencil down and began rubbing his eyes furiously with his menthol fingers. Big mistake.

"Oh my God, Jason's crying!" one of my

classmates exclaimed.

"No, I'm not!" Jason insisted, blinking furiously.

But it was too late. Everyone ran over and huddled next to Jason. It wasn't every day a kid in fifth grade started bawling — fourth grade maybe, but not fifth grade. We watched with wide eyes as Jason cried and cried. Sunlight flooded in through the tall glass windows, and Jason's tears glistened in the warm peach glow. I couldn't stop smiling the whole time.

It was a beautiful, beautiful day.

CHAPTER 41

The only thing that could make that day more beautiful was the chance of Lupe forgiving me. I watched as she read my letter and a smile bloomed across her face.

"So you'll do it? You'll enter the essay contest?" I asked her.

Lupe chuckled.

"Oh, no. If you want to win a motel, you're going to have to win it yourself," she said. "But I *will* help you with your grammar."

I threw my arms around her.

"And I'm sorry about what I said about you and Jason. You guys are not the same at all," Lupe said into my hair.

I skipped all the way home that day, riding the wave of hope and promise, a glorious wave so strong and powerful, I thought it would never end.

But then I turned onto Coast Boulevard.

Everything came crashing down. My

mother was lying by the side of the road. Blood, a thick, gooey red, gushed down the side of her face.

"Mom!" I screamed.

With her shivering hands, she touched her stomach, then stared at her fingertips, blinking in disbelief as she registered the color.

Shaking, she told me what happened. While I was at school, some people came and tried to break into the front office. They were after the cash register. My mom heard them and rushed downstairs. The first kick, to Mom's stomach, landed with a thud. She had screamed in pain and fallen to the ground.

My father was in the laundry room and couldn't hear her over the roar of the washing machine, but Hank heard the scream. He came running out of his room just as the second kick landed — to my mother's head.

"Oh, Mom!" I hugged her and cried.

Her lips were cut open, and she could barely talk.

"They took off running when they saw Hank," she cried. "But Hank ran after them. I'd never seen him so angry. He's still out there —"

Suddenly, I heard my dad's voice.

"Mia!" my father called.

I looked over at him. He was standing by the laundry room, carrying an armful of towels. When he saw my mother on the ground, the towels fell from his hands. He ran toward us.

The pain that whipped across his face when he got up close and saw my mom was indescribable. He collapsed on the ground next to her, his voice shaking as he told her it was going to be okay.

Carefully, I helped my mom up from the curb and brought her into the manager's quarters. We got her into bed, where I put an ice pack on her head and a hot-water bottle over her tummy. The wound had turned deep purple. Whenever I lifted the blanket to look, my mom grimaced.

My dad paced the living room.

"It should have been me, not you!" he said. "It should have been me!"

"I'm fine," my mom insisted, trying to sit up straighter, only to collapse back down because it was too painful.

"We have to take her to a hospital," I said to my dad.

"No," my mom said, coughing. "We don't have any insurance. Going to the hospital will kill us."

My dad plunged his head into his hands. I realized he was crying. "How did we get here?" he muttered over and over again. "How did we get here?"

I walked over to my room and retrieved my ziplock bag of tips.

"I have some money," I said. My parents were so busy crying and coughing, they didn't even hear me.

"You guys! *I have some money!*" I yelled.

My father drove as quickly as he could. "Hang on!" he said. "We're almost there!"

I sat in the back clutching my ziplock bag full of money with one hand and holding my mother with the other.

The doctor in the ER saw my mom right away. He was a white guy and seemed really concerned. He asked my mom whether she was dizzy. She said no. He asked my mom whether she remembered blacking out when she hit the ground. She said maybe, she wasn't sure. He asked her to describe the pain on a scale of one to ten. I thought for sure she would say ten or even eleven, from the way she kept grinding her teeth and wincing every time she moved, but she insisted it was more like a seven.

They took her in for an X-ray. My dad and I waited outside because they said it wasn't good for kids to be in the X-ray room.

When at last the doctor reappeared, he had good news. None of Mom's bones were broken. She had a mild concussion, and the doctor gave her painkillers and bandages for the bleeding (which thankfully was just on the outside, not the inside).

"Make sure she takes it easy the next few days," he said. "Use an ice pack for ten to twenty minutes at a time. Gradually, the swelling will go down and so will the bruising. No work. No gym."

My dad laughed out loud when he said *gym*. I guess the idea of my mom (or any of us) going to the gym was pretty funny. My dad promised she wouldn't and thanked the doc.

His smile faded when the doctor gave him the bill. I peeked around his arm and read the paper too: The total came out to $5,800. My dad gripped the counter to keep from falling — I thought *he* was going to have a concussion. Frantically, he explained to the nurses in his broken English that we didn't have any insurance.

"No insurance?" the nurses asked exasperatedly. "How could you have no insurance?"

The nurses stared long and hard at us, these alien, insuranceless creatures. They told us to wait while they got their supervisor.

Ten minutes later, the supervisor appeared. He was another white guy, stern-looking, about forty years old. As we explained our insuranceless situation to him, he looked like he had about as much empathy as a LEGO. He asked us to fill out a bunch of special forms for low-income people.

"We'll only waive the hospital bills if you make less than the federal poverty income guideline for a family of three," he said.

We started filling out the forms. Since my parents made about $750 a month, that came out to $9,000 a year. The poverty line for a family our size was $11,890. So we were well below the poverty line, but the form also asked us how much we paid in rent. We put down $0, because technically, we got free board living in the manager's quarters.

The supervisor looked at that and started shaking his head.

"Free rent? I'm sorry, but I don't think you qualify," he said.

"What do you mean?" my mom asked.

"You can't get free rent *and* free health care," he said, crossing his arms.

"But we're dirt poor!" I said. "It says so right here."

I held up the poverty chart on the form

237

he gave us. There it was, clear as day, how categorically poor we were.

He took a long look at us.

"I bet you guys aren't even citizens."

We looked at the floor.

"No."

"Didn't think so. You'll have to take it up with Billing and Collections. They'll decide whether you qualify for full waiver or not. But I doubt it," he said. "Until then, the most I can give you is a forty percent discount. So you'll still need to pay . . ."

He pulled out a calculator and started crunching the numbers.

"Three thousand four hundred and eighty dollars," he announced.

At this point, my mom started crying.

She let out a sob so thunderous, I wondered if my cousins in China could hear her. I've never seen her cry like that before, not even when she was lying on the side of the street. The doctor who had been examining her ran over to see what was wrong. When I explained the situation to him, he turned angrily to the hospital supervisor.

"You want to charge these poor people three thousand four hundred and eighty dollars? Can't you see they just *got* the crap beat out of them?" he asked the supervisor, almost yelling.

The supervisor looked sheepish but insisted on having a word with the doctor in private.

We held our breaths as the two of them walked into a room and closed the door. We could see them arguing through the glass window. The doctor's arms kept flying and the supervisor's head kept shaking. When they came out, my father held my hand so tight it hurt. The supervisor spoke first.

"We've decided . . . in light of the circumstances . . ." he started to say.

"We're going to waive the fees," the doctor blurted out.

"Really?" my mom asked. She peered at the doctor with her big brown bruised eyes.

"Really," the doctor said. I threw my arms around him. My mother collapsed into my dad.

The supervisor cleared his throat. "There's still a basic hospital fee of a hundred and fifty dollars you'll need to pay," he said.

I held up my ziplock bag, full of dollar bills and quarters.

"I've got that right here."

I'd be lying if I said it didn't hurt, handing over my ziplock bag. All those nights I stayed up secretly counting the money with a flashlight, the adrenaline and excitement coursing through me. In a flash it was all gone. But another part of me felt tremendously proud, to be able to pay for our first visit to the doctor in this country with money I'd earned all by myself.

When we got home, my dad and I helped my mom into my bed. We thought it would be a good idea for her to sleep there for a while so that she wouldn't be jolted awake at night by the sound of the front desk buzzer.

"How come you didn't you tell us you had all this money?" my mom asked.

I shrugged.

"Well, thank you, honey," my mom said. She put her arms around me and hugged me tight. "Thank you for spending it on your old mom."

My dad came in and set down the tea, bathing the room in jasmine.

"Get some sleep," my dad said to my mom, kissing the top of her head.

My mom reached for my dad's hand.

"Hey," my mom said to my dad. "Thanks for taking me to the hospital."

My dad turned away from her.

"What's wrong?" my mom asked him.

He shook his head. He had great big teardrops in his eyes.

"What is it?" my mother asked softly.

"I promised when I married you that I'd take care of you," he said in a small voice. "And I've failed you."

I sucked in a breath. I looked over at my mom, who sat there calmly, a hand draped casually over her wound.

"Quit feeling so sorry for yourself," my mom said to my dad. "*I'll* decide when you've failed me. And you're not even close."

In that moment, I realized how deep my parents' love for each other was. It was deeper than anything Mr. Yao or America could throw at them.

My dad chuckled and kissed my mom's bruised lips.

"What did I ever do to deserve you?" he asked.

That night, I did not go to sleep. I stayed up late waiting for Hank to come home and writing a letter to the doctor who helped my mom.

Dear Doctor,

Thank you for helping my mom. She's sleeping now. She asked before she fell asleep if ~~there are~~ there was any more stinky tofu in the cupboard, so I think

241

she's going to be okay.

~~Your~~ You're the first doctor we've ever seen in America. ~~Honest~~ To be honest, I was always a little scared of you. My parents said we should never ever see you, unless we were seriously ~~gonna~~ about to die, and even ~~than~~ then, we should think about it.

That's because you're really expensive. I always thought that made you ~~kinda~~ kind of mean. But tonight, I learned you're not mean at all. In fact, you're very kind.

Thank you for not charging my mom all that money. Thank you for showing us ~~its~~ it's not just every man for himself in America. I hope to ~~in the future~~ one day be able to ~~return~~ repay you. Until then, I hope you'll accept this letter and this picture of a tree that I drew for you. The tree ~~is~~ represents my mom and the leaves represent all the new hope you've given her that people in America are kind.

Sincerely,
Mia Tang

All night, I worked on the tree, making little *v*'s for branches and twigs just as Lupe had taught me. I then drew leaves, hundreds and hundreds of little leaves, not rushing this time, because the doctor did not rush with my mom. He took his time.

It was 3:00 a.m. when I finally finished. Hank still wasn't home.

From the lumpy living room sofa, I peered out the window at the dark, eerie streets. I wondered what happened to him. Did he find those people? Did they hurt him?

The worry festered in me until morning when I couldn't stand it any longer and told my dad we had to do something. Go to the police. Start searching the streets.

Just as we were about to head out, Hank came limping back, wearing the same clothes as yesterday, his hair a disheveled mess.

"What happened?" I asked him.

Hank sighed.

"You want the good news or the bad news?" he asked.

CHAPTER 42

The good news was the punks got arrested, Hank told us. My mom put a hand over her chest and sighed with relief.

"The bad news is so did I," Hank muttered.

"What?" I lunged forward. "That's terrible!"

Hank chased the guys who beat up my mom five blocks. As he was running, Hank picked up a rock and threw it at them. The rock landed on the guy's head and they got into a huge fight. A cop parked across the street saw what happened and immediately jumped out of his car and arrested them all. Hank was charged with assault with a deadly weapon and had to spend the night in jail.

My mom covered her mouth with her hands.

"Oh my God, I'm so sorry," my mom said.

"Where are the other guys?" I asked.

"They're still in jail. But I took the plea and at least now I'm out," he said.

My mom reached over and put her hand on top of Hank's.

"Oh, Hank," my mom said.

Hank looked at her.

"What about you — you okay?" he asked. "What'd the doctor say?"

"He said I'll be fine. It's just a concussion," my mom told him.

"What about the bleeding?" he asked.

"It's only on the outside," my mom said, touching her bandage with her hand.

Hank nodded, relieved to hear. "Good," he said. "Now if you'll excuse me, I gotta go to my room and pack."

"What for?" I asked.

"I can't stay here rent free anymore," he said. "I spent the night in jail, remember? I've broken my thirty days."

"By one day!" I exclaimed.

"Still," Hank said. "Rules are rules."

"Mr. Yao's not going to know."

Hank looked at the floor.

"When I was in jail, they put two and two together. They remembered me from the car theft case. So they called up Mr. Yao and told him I was in jail," he said with a sigh. "He knows."

Hank lifted his eyes to meet mine.

"Take care of your mom, kiddo," he said.

A lump formed in my throat seeing him standing there empty-handed, with no money, no place to live, and nowhere to go.

"You can't leave!" I said.

I looked to my parents.

"Mia's right," my dad said. "We have to do something."

CHAPTER 43

Hank was shocked by our offer.

"Hide me? Are you sure?"

"Yes," my parents said. "We do it all the time for immigrants from China. We just have to be careful."

"What if we get caught?" Hank asked.

"We won't tell if you don't tell," my mom said.

We helped Hank clean out his stuff and move into another room. There was no way he could keep staying in room 12 — Mr. Yao might go and check in there. He had to switch rooms, but not with so much stuff. Hank had a lot of junk that he'd accumulated over the years, so whatever he decided wasn't essential, we chucked. We moved his tomato plant to the pool. The rest we moved into my closet. When he was able to get his bare essentials down to one small bag, my dad handed him the key to room 5.

"It'll only be for a little while," Hank said.

"Just until I get back on my feet."

He was adamant about finding another job. On that front, he wasn't having a ton of luck, though. The problem wasn't finding an open position; it was that he didn't have a reference letter from his old employer.

"What's a reference letter?" I asked him before I left for the night. He didn't seem like he wanted to talk about it much, so he wouldn't say exactly. Just that it was important and he didn't have it.

Later that week, I asked Hank if there was anything I could do to help him find a job, but again, he batted me away.

"Look, if it was simple, I would have asked you already. But it's not. It's complicated," he said.

"What's so complicated about it?" I asked him.

He shook his head.

"You're just a kid. You wouldn't understand," he said. Which hurt. A lot.

I wanted to say to Hank, *No,* you *don't understand! You don't understand what it's like to have to hold in your pee and not make a sound when you're in the bathroom, and the popular girls walk in and start talking about you.*

I crossed my arms at Hank. "Try me," I said.

He sighed.

"Most places won't hire you unless you have a letter from your old boss saying how good you were. And I don't have that," he said, frowning.

"Well, could you get it?" I asked him.

He shook his head.

"No. I already tried." He paused for a second and added, "And that's not even the biggest problem."

"What's the biggest problem?" I asked.

"The biggest problem is that on top of everything else, now I have a criminal conviction."

His fight with the guys who beat up my mom meant he had a record now — no employer wanted to touch him.

"I can't even hide it," he said. "All they have to do is run a criminal record check and boom, there it is!"

"So tell them the truth," I said. "Tell them you were defending my mom."

"They'll never believe that," he said.

"Why not?"

Hank shook his head.

"Because I'm not like you, Mia. People look at you and they see a nice, sweet Chinese girl."

"What do they see when they see you?" I asked.

He looked at his feet.

"A criminal," Hank said.

"No," I said firmly. "Don't say that!"

"Why do you think I took the plea? I know what the verdict would be if we went to trial. People look at me and see guilty."

I shook my head furiously. "No, no," I kept repeating.

Hank got quiet.

"There are some things, Mia, that no matter how hard you try, you'll never fully understand."

As Hank looked into my eyes, I realized there were reference letters and mean girls. And then there were other things on a whole other level of "you don't understand."

CHAPTER 44

The police came over two days after the robbery to get my mom's statement about her attackers. She was worried about having to testify in court because of her broken English, but the police officers assured her she didn't need to testify if she didn't want to. Her attackers were ex-convicts who had skipped out on their parole. They were going to stay in jail, this time with no parole. My mother was relieved.

Word got out about my mother's attack, and the security guard from the Topaz Inn once again came bopping over. Hank and I were both at the front desk this time.

I narrowed my eyes. "What do you want?"

"I heard about the attack," he said. "Terrible, just terrible. Too bad you guys didn't have a security guard like me. I would have pounded his head in."

"And you would have gotten arrested," Hank pointed out.

The security guard gave a half shrug.

"In my line of work, an arrest is a badge of courage," he said. He jammed his hands into his pocket and pulled out a business card.

"Here's my number in case you guys ever need to hire a security guard," he said, sliding his card across the desk.

I picked it up and was about to throw it away, when Hank said, "Let me see that." He took the card with him back to his room.

The next morning, Hank came back to the front office with four letters. He handed them to me.

"Mail these for me, will you?" he asked.

"Sure thing," I said, taking the letters from him.

The envelopes were addressed to various malls in our area, Anaheim Plaza (where my mom and I liked to go), the Garden Walk, the Festival over in Anaheim Hills (which was supposed to be really nice), and Canyon Plaza.

One of the envelopes was not sealed tight, and as I flipped it over, the letter fell out. The words *security guard* caught my eye. I started reading.

Dear Anaheim Plaza,
    My name is Hank Caleb, and I would

like to apply for a job as a security guard in your mall. I am hardworking and honest. I am also responsible and take my job very seriously. My last job was working at a gas station — I had to do many things like tend to the cash register, keep an eye on the customers (a lot of people try to steal from gas stations), wash windshields, and check fluid levels and air pressure.

During my entire time working at the gas station, I was never late once. I take great pride in my work, and I would like the opportunity to be a security guard because I like helping people and keeping them safe. If you hire me, I will not let you down.

I would be honored to come in for an interview.

Sincerely,
Hank Caleb

I thought it was a wonderful letter, and as I read it, I wanted to run out the back, find Hank, and give him a hug. I hoped they gave him an interview and didn't just write back asking for a reference letter. I started thinking some more about this pesky reference letter. If only there was a way I could help him get one.

That's when it dawned on me.

I got out a piece of paper and started writing.

Dear ~~boss~~ employer,

I would like to ~~recomand~~ recommend Hank Caleb to you as a security guard. Hank Caleb has been a security guard at the Calivista Motel from June until now, and he is the ~~best~~ most responsible, ~~good~~ capable, and ~~brave~~ courageous security guard we ~~has~~ have ever had. Recently, at the Calivista, we had ~~a~~ an ~~awful~~ unfortunate ~~thing~~ incident ~~on~~ in which some ~~crazy~~ dangerous people tried to steal money from the cash register. One of our managers tried to stop them and was beaten up and had to go to the hospital. Hank ~~right away~~ immediately ran after the ~~crazy people~~ attackers. He chased them four blocks. He managed to catch them and he got into a fight with them.

Unfortunately, some cops saw Hank getting into a fight with them and he ended up ~~in jail~~ arrested, but the point is, Hank ~~did a LOT~~ went out of his way to protect his managers, when most security guards would have ~~chickened out~~ stayed back.

You will not find a better security

guard ~~then~~ than Hank. Please find the receipt of the hospital bill stapled as ~~proof~~ evidence. If you have any questions, please call the Calivista at 555-281-0482.

Sincerely,
The Managers of the Calivista Motel

It took me two and a half hours and five drafts to write the reference letter. I didn't want the letter to sound like it came from a kid, so I borrowed Mrs. T's dictionary-thesaurus again, and tried to make it as good as Hank's. I substituted simple words for fancier words and checked all the tenses and grammar. Finally, after proofreading it ten times, I copied the letter onto four clean white sheets of paper. I also rewrote Hank's letters — in a different handwriting — and changed all the stuff he wrote about working at a gas station to working at the Calivista. As I was forging Hank's signature, I felt a teeny tiny bit bad. Was what I was doing wrong? What if I got caught? Would Hank be mad at me?

Part of me wanted to go over and tell Hank what I was doing, ask him if it was okay, but the other part of me worried he would say no, especially given his strict views on reference letters. As I fretted over what to do, I glanced over at my math textbook and thought of my mom.

She told me once when she was a little girl, she would eavesdrop on her brother's math lessons with his tutor. Her family only had enough money for one math tutor to come by the house and her parents did not think it was useful to educate a girl. But my mother, because she loved math so much, refused to give up. She would listen in on her brother's lesson every week. If the tutor assigned homework, she would secretly do the homework. And here's the funny part: She would then sneak over to her brother's desk at night and change all her brother's answers to match her own so that when the tutor came, he'd go over with him what *she* did wrong.

In time, my mother got really good at math. That's probably why she was constantly hounding me to do more math. But that wasn't the point. The point was sometimes, you have to take matters into your own hands. And you have to be creative to get what you want.

I stuffed the letters into new envelopes. As I licked them shut, I whispered under my breath, *"Please let this work."*

CHAPTER 45

As the autumn leaves turned and Hank waited to hear back from the malls, we got a surprise visitor: a kid. You'd think that since we were so close to Disneyland, we got a lot of kids, but we didn't. People with children preferred to stay at the actual Disneyland Hotel or the nicer hotels over in Anaheim Hills. We did get the occasional teenager, traveling with his parent, grumbling about not getting his own room. We also got the occasional toddler, pitter-pattering around the parking lot, happily sucking on her thumb.

But sadly, not many kids my age. So it was pretty cool when I looked up one day and saw a girl standing in front of the front desk with her mom. She had a mane of bright red hair and freckles across her nose.

"Hi! I'm Mia!" I said eagerly.

Unfortunately, the girl did not return my enthusiasm. She chewed her gum loudly and looked at me like I was a bonus question on a math test.

I handed her mom a registration form.

"So are you guys on vacation?" I asked while her mom filled out the form.

No response.

"We're only two miles from Disneyland," I said. "Just keep going on Coast and you'll hit the freeway —"

"We know where Disneyland is," the girl snapped.

She turned to her mom. "Are you done yet?" she asked. She stuck her hands into the pockets of her skinny jeans. She was wearing Calvin Klein jeans, the kind I would kill for. Her mother tossed me back the form.

As the two of them took their key and turned toward the door, I called after them, "If you need anything —"

"We won't!" the girl shouted, slamming the door behind her. Talk about rude.

I called Lupe up on the phone later to complain. "You won't believe this girl," I said. "*So* rude."

"Did she fall off the mean tree and hit every branch on the way down?" Lupe asked.

I giggled. "You and your trees!" I pictured Lupe sitting in her room, her walls lined with drawings of trees.

"You know, I've still never been to your house," I pointed out to her.

"Ah, it's not much to look at," she said.

That wasn't the point.

"Are you gonna have me over?"

"Yeah."

"When?"

"Soon."

I woke up the next morning to the most unexpected surprise. My mother ran into my room holding a pair of jeans.

"Guess what? The girl and her mom left and they left behind these!" my mom squealed. She tossed me the jeans. "They *might* just fit you! What do you say? You want to try these on after we wash them?"

I jumped out of bed, and the two of us raced to the laundry room. My mother threw the jeans in for a spin. I sat with my nose pressed up against the washer. This was it! No more ugly floral pants. No more standing out like a sore thumb. I was getting my very first pair of American jeans!

They were warm when they came out of the dryer. I held the jeans up to my face, closed my eyes, and smelled.

They smelled like hope.

The new jeans fit me like a glove. One-hundred-percent normal hugging my legs. I put on a nice shirt and practically skipped to school. Jason arched an eyebrow when I walked past. So did the popular girls in my class.

I tried to play it cool, of course. I tried to walk normally, one foot in front of the other, but inside me, fireworks were going off.

CHAPTER 46

I wore my new jeans to school every single day, and every evening, I put them in the washer and waited around in my pajamas while they dried. I didn't dare let them out of my sight. I was waiting around for my jeans to dry one night when Hank ran into the laundry room. It was the day before Thanksgiving, and he had the biggest smile on his face I'd ever seen.

"You're looking at the new security guard down at the mall," he said proudly.

"Oh my God!" I shrieked.

"It worked! The letter worked!" he said.

Confetti cannons went off inside me.

"You know what else worked? *Your* letter," he added. I immediately tensed up. Was he mad?

Hank chuckled and patted me on the back.

"It was bold, I'll tell you that much," he said. "But hey, they bought it!"

Phew.

"How did you find out?"

"It was the first thing they asked me about. Tell us about working as a security guard at the Calivista," he said.

"And? What'd you say?" I asked him.

"I said I'd never worked with nicer people," he said. "And I meant it."

I smiled.

"Can't believe you did that," Hank said, shaking his head. "What possessed you?"

I took his hand and led him over to the front office, where I grabbed Lupe's card, the one that said *You can't win if you don't play.*

I handed it to him. Hank looked down at the card and pulled me in for a bear hug.

That Thanksgiving, we invited all the weeklies into the manager's quarters to celebrate. It was our first real Thanksgiving, and even though my mom didn't know how to make turkey, she knew how to make turkey sandwiches. And buy a premade apple pie from Ralphs. Hank brought cherry tomatoes from his tomato plant too. As the sweet and tangy smells of apple pie and cherry tomatoes and buttery toast filled the manager's quarters, we all went around the table and said what we were thankful for.

"I'm thankful your mom's okay," my dad said, his eyes smiling at my mom.

"Hear, hear," everyone agreed.

"I'm thankful for my new job," Hank said. He raised his cream soda to me and said, "Thank you, Mia."

I smiled.

"What about you, Mia?" Mrs. Q asked. "What are you thankful for?"

I looked at everyone, at all the love in the room.

"I'm thankful for you guys," I said.

CHAPTER 47

With Hank making money again, we no longer had to hide him. Mr. Yao was baffled when he found out what happened.

"How did that deadbeat sneak back in here?" he wanted to know. Still, money was money and Mr. Yao was happy to take Hank's now that he had it.

Hank was happy too, for it meant he could roam around the motel freely again. When I got home from school, I found him sitting up on the roof with Lupe's dad.

"Whatcha doin up there?" I called.

"I was just helping José here with his tools," Hank said.

I looked at José, who seemed very happy to have some company up there on the roof.

"Want to hang out at the desk?" Hank asked.

"No, it's okay," I said. "Stay. I'll get you guys some sodas."

■ ■ ■ ■

As Hank and José sipped sodas on the roof,
I went back to the front desk. There were
four messages waiting for me. Aunt Ling,
Uncle Zhu, Aunt Ping, and Uncle Yang had
called to say they went by the addresses I
gave them, but none of them had seen the
missing Thunderbird. That meant we were
down to the final address — the home of
Mrs. Robinson.

Oh God, I hope they don't find the car there.
Sometimes, when I wanted something
really bad, I'd ask myself what I would be
willing to give up for it. For example, when
I was waiting in the hospital that day my
mom got beat up, I asked myself what I
would be willing to give up for my mom to
be okay. I decided I would be willing to give
up the essay contest. I'd rather be stuck on
a bad roller coaster with my mom, than on
a good roller coaster all by myself.

Today, as I thought about Mrs. Robinson
and what I would give for it not to be her, I
looked down at my new jeans. I decided I
would be willing to give them up just to
prove Mr. Yao wrong.

I looked up from my jeans to see a Chinese
man running into the motel. He came by

foot. He didn't have a car, which was odd for California. As soon as my mom saw him, she dropped her mop.

"Xiao Zhang!" she cried.

"Xiao Ying!" he exclaimed, the warmth of their affection coming through in their greeting. Xiao meant *little* in Chinese and was something you called dear friends. They hugged each other and jumped with joy.

At dinner, I learned that Uncle Zhang and my mom used to work together in China. They were both engineers.

"Uncle Zhang was one of the best engineers we had. He can fix a television in thirty seconds," my mom said, picking up slices of ham with her chopsticks and adding them to his plate.

"Well, more like a minute," Uncle Zhang said. He and my mom laughed.

"So when did you get here?" my dad asked.

"About a year ago," Uncle Zhang said.

My mother asked him what he had been doing. That's when Uncle Zhang dropped his chopsticks.

"I don't know how to say this, but I . . . I . . ." He shook his head.

"What?" my mom asked. "What is it?"

Uncle Zhang's eyes watered.

"Oh, Ying, I'm in an awful mess," he said quietly.

Slowly, he began to tell us what happened. Shortly after he came to America, he got a job working in a kitchen. The employer was an American guy and told all the workers that their passports and IDs would be safer with him. So he took them all away.

Without their passports and IDs, the workers had no way to leave. Month after excruciating month, they put up with long hours, toiling away in a hot kitchen with virtually no pay.

"We work eighteen hours a day, from six a.m. to midnight. We only get one day off a month," Uncle Zhang said.

At night, Uncle Zhang and the other workers slept at the employer's house, in a basement with no windows.

"I'm basically a slave," he cried. "I only got out today because Immigration came and raided us, so everyone had to flee through the secret tunnels!"

"What secret tunnels??" I asked.

He told us that inside the restaurant there was a closet in the kitchen with a white apron. Behind the white apron, there was a button. If you pushed the button, the closet wall would open up and you could crawl out. The secret tunnels led to hiding places and directly outside.

"We never thought it would happen but today, Immigration showed up," Uncle Zhang said.

As soon as the Immigration officers walked through the door, one of the waitresses came into the kitchen and put in an order for "Ice Fried Rice" — that was the code word. One by one, Uncle Zhang and the other workers slipped inside the closet and crawled out through the tunnels.

"When I got out, I kept looking up at the sky, so vast and blue," Uncle Zhang said. "It'd been ages since I'd seen the light of day."

"And how did you manage to find us?" my mom asked.

"Oh, that part was easy! Every Chinese waiter up and down the coast of California knows about this place. Look out for the blue cap, they say. You guys are famous!" Uncle Zhang said with a wink.

Then Uncle Zhang's face fell, and he got real quiet. "But I have to go back. They still have my passport and ID."

My mom shook her head. "There's got to be something you can do." Uncle Zhang shook his head right back.

"It's my own fault," he said. "I should never have taken the job in the first place."

"Why did you?"

"Because I was desperate . . ."
Uncle Zhang swallowed hard.
"I got into some trouble with loan sharks."

Chapter 48

Uncle Zhang had borrowed $500 from some loan sharks when he first came to America, just as Uncle Ming had.

"It wasn't even for myself. It was for my mom back home. She was very sick and I thought . . . I thought . . ." He could barely finish.

"You thought maybe if you paid for an expensive doctor, she might get better," my dad said, glancing at my mom. My mom slipped her hand into his.

Uncle Zhang shook his head.

"It wasn't even that. She had stage four cancer. It had already spread. There was nothing they could do," he said.

"So then . . . ?"

His eyes grew moist, his voice shaky.

"I borrowed the money so she could die knowing her only son was okay out there. That I had made it in America. Instead of the loser . . ."

Uncle Zhang started crying.

"Listen to me. You're not a loser," my dad said. "None of us knew it was going to be like this."

"I couldn't even say good-bye." Uncle Zhang bit down on his lower lip. "I was afraid if I called her, she'd hear it in my voice how much I was struggling. So I refused. No matter how many times she asked for me in the end, I refused to get on the phone with her."

My mom put a hand on Uncle Zhang's shoulder. None of us said a word. I sat very still, thinking about my own secrets that I was keeping from my parents, my missing pencil, the C-minus lurking in my closet. I thought about my parents and how they almost never wanted to call or write to my grandparents or Shen's family. And *if* we called them, my mother always rushed to get off the phone. Either that or she'd put on the same voice she used at Macy's when she said, "Just looking."

As the hazy sky turned into night, my parents, Uncle Zhang, and I gazed out the window, thinking of all the things we wanted to say to our parents but couldn't.

In the middle of the night, I got out of bed and went over to my mom and dad's bed.

My dad was snoring peacefully.

I hesitated for just a second — he got so little sleep, my dad — before shaking him awake.

"Dad," I whispered.

"Huh? Did a customer come?" he asked, jerking his eyes open and sitting up. "I'll be right there!"

"No, Dad, it's just me," I said. "I can't sleep. I keep thinking about Uncle Zhang and his passport."

"I know," my dad sighed. "Me too."

"What's he going to do?"

"I don't know, honey," my dad said. "Hopefully he can meet someone soon who can help him."

"Like who?"

"A lawyer maybe," my dad said.

"What can a lawyer do for him?" I asked.

My dad thought about it.

"A lawyer will be able to tell his employer what's what," he said.

"Well, why can't we tell people what's what?" I asked him.

He chuckled.

"We can, sweetheart, but nobody's going to listen to us," he said.

That's not true, I thought. *Hank's new employer, he listened.*

My dad rolled back on his side.

"There's nothing you can do, sweetheart," he said. "Now try to get some sleep."

I went back to my room, but I didn't get some sleep. Instead, I pulled out a piece of paper from my drawer and Mrs. T's big old dictionary-thesaurus, which I still had from when I wrote Hank's letter. With a flashlight, I started writing.

Dear employer,

I am writing to you about your employee Zhang Xiling. Mr. Zhang ~~says~~ has ~~told~~ informed me that you ~~have~~ are in possession of his passport and ID. It is ~~wrong~~ illegal to ~~take away~~ confiscate someone's passport and ID. ~~You gotta give it back!~~ I request your ~~quick~~ immediate return of Mr. Zhang's passport and ID. ~~If you don't do it, you'll be sorry.~~ Failure to do so will result in ~~big trouble~~ serious consequences. ~~And don't lie and say you did because I'm gonna ask Mr. Zhang!~~ I will be ~~asking~~ following up with Mr. Zhang to see if you have returned his passport and ID. Thank you for your attention.

Sincerely,
Mia Tang,
Lawyer

I worked on the letter all night long, making sure the tone, punctuation, and syntax was all right. I read it over five times and when I was pretty sure I had corrected all the grammatical mistakes, I copied it onto a clean sheet of white paper.

Before I left for school, I handed Uncle Zhang the letter. "This is for you," I told him. "I don't know if it'll work, but it's worth a shot." I watched as his eyes danced across my writing.

"You *wrote* this?" he asked.

"Well, I had a thesaurus," I said.

"Mia, this is incredible," he said.

I blushed.

"I hope it works for you, Uncle Zhang," I said, hugging him.

"Me too," he said, clutching the letter. "Me too."

CHAPTER 49

After Uncle Zhang left, we got a call from one of the other immigrants. He had been over to Mrs. Robinson's house, and the stolen neon green Ford Thunderbird was not there!

I looked down at my lucky jeans and thought, *Phew.*

With the car officially nowhere to be found, I felt it was only appropriate I personally tell the owner, Mr. Lorenz. So I opened up the ledger, looked up his phone number, and gave him a call. When he didn't pick up, I glanced at his address and was surprised to see that he lived right here in Anaheim, a couple blocks from my school, actually.

After school, Lupe and I went over to his house. Mr. Lorenz lived in a small yellow house on Orange Avenue. We walked up and knocked on the door.

"Hello? Mr. Lorenz?" I called. "Anyone home?"

Lupe cupped her hands and tried to peer through the window.

We heard rustling and footsteps. Finally, the door opened a crack.

"Who's asking?" Mr. Lorenz said.

"It's me, Mia, the girl from the Calivista? Where your car got stolen?" I said. "And this is my friend Lupe."

Lupe waved at Mr. Lorenz. "Hey," she said.

"Can we come in?" I asked him.

Mr. Lorenz didn't let us in right away. He paused to think about it, and then, finally, he sighed and undid the chain to his door.

His house had a funky smell, like somebody had been cooking stinky tofu and forgot to open the window. Lupe wrinkled her nose as we took a seat on the couch.

"This better be quick," Mr. Lorenz said.

"Don't worry, this will only take a minute," I said. "I just wanted to come over and tell you personally that we can't find your car."

"That's okay. The insurance company has already comped me," he said.

"I know. But still, it's important you know —"

"Is that it?" Mr. Lorenz snapped.

Just then, we heard a loud *vroom*. A car came speeding down the road and parked right in front of Mr. Lorenz's house. We glanced out the window. Our eyes stretched when we registered the color: neon green.

"Hey, isn't that —" Lupe asked.

Yes, yes, it was. It was a neon green Thunderbird. *The* neon green Thunderbird!

The driver of the car got up and walked up to the house. He turned the doorknob.

"Hey, man, you said the car was in perfect condition, but the windshield's got all these dents in it," the guy said, tossing the keys to Mr. Lorenz. Then he looked at us.

"Who are you?" he asked.

"We're just . . ." Lupe said.

"Leaving!" I announced. I grabbed Lupe's hand and lunged for the door, but Mr. Lorenz was quicker than me.

He slammed the door shut with one hand.

"Not so fast," he said. "Where do you two think you're going?"

"Home," I said. I glanced at Lupe. Sweat beads were falling like raindrops from her forehead. "We gotta go home and do our homework, right, Lupe?"

"Yeah! We have *a lot* of homework."

"And when you're done doing your homework, what are you going to say?" Mr. Lorenz asked. He leaned into us. I could feel the hairs rising on my neck. "About what you saw?"

My breath caught in my throat.

"Nothing!" I said. "I didn't see anything!"

"Me neither!" Lupe said.

He stared at us. Desperately, I tried to erase my thoughts so he couldn't read them.

"Good," he said, his wet lips twisted into a smirk. He crouched down and whispered into our ears, "Breathe a word about this to anyone and I will come and find you."

The threat grabbed me and smothered me as I ran all the way home.

CHAPTER 50

I sat at the front desk waiting for Hank to get home. He and Fred had gone to an Angels baseball game. It was getting to be rush hour. I stared at the cars crawling down Coast Boulevard, muttering "C'mon, c'mon" under my breath. When at last I spotted Hank's pickup coming down the road, I ran outside waving my arms.

Breathlessly, I told him and Fred what happened.

"I knew it!" Hank said, throwing his Angels baseball cap onto the ground. "What'd I tell you, Fred? It was an inside job. The guy probably thought he could pull a thirty-day special!"

"What's a thirty-day special?" I asked.

"A thirty-day special is when someone reports his car got stolen, but it's not really stolen," Fred said. "He's just hiding it for thirty days."

My mind was swarming with questions.

"Why thirty days?"

"Because that's how long most insurance companies take to settle the claim," Hank explained. "The insurance company probably gave him a big fat check for the price of his car."

"And what happens to the car?"

Hank shrugged. "He could try to sell it to someone or sell it for parts."

"That's probably what he was doing when we went over there," I said. "We have to call the police!"

I grabbed the phone and dialed the number for Officer Phillips.

This time, Officer Phillips actually listened. He and his colleagues went straight over to Mr. Lorenz's house, where they watched him for a while and eventually caught him red-handed trying to sell his stolen car. They arrested him on the spot for insurance fraud, money laundering, and a whole bunch of other bad stuff I'd never even heard of before.

"He'll be going away for a long, long time," Officer Phillips said when he came over later that night.

That was a relief considering the last thing Mr. Lorenz said to me.

Officer Phillips shook my hand and

thanked me for "cracking the case." I was all smiles. My mom and dad joked that maybe I could get a job on the force one day. Officer Phillips chuckled and was about to turn to leave when I nudged him and pointed toward Hank's room. Officer Phillips sighed but he followed me over. Hank answered on the first knock, then frowned when he saw who it was. Officer Phillips looked similarly unthrilled, but nevertheless he muttered an apology for having wrongly accused Hank.

"You know what that cost me? It cost me my job!" Hank said.

"Again, I'm sorry," Officer Phillips said flatly.

Hank looked him straight in the eye.

"Don't be sorry. Be better," Hank said. "Next time you accuse a black man, stop and think."

Officer Phillips looked away and didn't say anything.

That night, my mother and father came into my room.

"We're proud of you," they said.

"Even though you went into a stranger's house," my mom tsk-tsked, but I could tell she wasn't really mad.

They took a seat at the foot of my bed, and my mother reached for my hand.

"Do you still remember asking me a while back why we came to America?" she asked.

I nodded.

"This is why," she said.

"Because of thirty-day specials?" I asked.

My mom chuckled and shook her head.

"No, sweetheart," she said. "Because here people are innocent until proven guilty. For the most part, at least. That's what you saw tonight."

Slowly, my parents started telling me about something that happened in China a long, long time ago called the Cultural Revolution. The Cultural Revolution was a political movement that took place in China in the 1960s and '70s. My parents said that during the Cultural Revolution, my grandparents were locked up and shipped away. It didn't matter whether they actually did anything wrong.

"That's why we left, so that something like that wouldn't happen to you," my dad said. "Tonight, seeing that police officer arrest Mr. Lorenz and actually come back here and apologize to Hank — okay, he didn't really want to apologize, but still, he did — I know I made the right decision. America may not be perfect, but she's free. And that makes all the difference."

I finally understood what my parents meant by "free."

CHAPTER 51

I hopped and skipped over to the Topaz Inn the next afternoon to tell the security guard the good news.

"You can rip up that ridiculous list of yours," I told him. But he just shrugged.

"Better safe than sorry," he said.

"But I just told you! Hank didn't do it. Neither did Mrs. Robinson or any of the other black customers. Mr. Lorenz did it. He's the one you should put on your list!"

No matter what I said, though, the crazy security guard refused to get rid of his list. He kept saying, "It's a free country. I can do whatever I want."

I wanted to shake him and say, *You're not getting it! That's not what "free" means! Free means innocent until proven guilty, not guilty no matter how innocent.*

I stormed back to the Calivista.

Hank was in the parking lot chatting with some customers. As soon as he saw my face, he asked, "What's wrong?"

He followed me inside the front office, and I told him what happened. "What do we do?" I asked him.

Hank didn't say anything for a long time. Then he reached across the front desk and grabbed a blank piece of paper.

"Do what you do best," he said, putting the paper in front of me.

"Will you help me?" I asked Hank.

Hank nodded. "Sure," he said.

That afternoon, we worked together on the letter. I wrote most of it but Hank helped me with certain key words, like "discriminatory," a word I did not know before.

Dear stores,

I know that the security guard from the Topaz Inn gave you a list of "bad customers." But it is not actually a list of bad customers. It is a list of black customers. He ~~puts~~ put them on the list because he ~~seem~~ seems to think that all black customers are bad. But that's (1) not true and (2) incredibly ~~mean~~ discriminatory.

I know it is not true because my good friend is black and he is one of the kindest people I know. Also, I just solved a case ~~involve~~ involving a stolen car and guess what? The thief was not black. Actually, he wasn't even a thief. He was the owner. That just goes to show — you shouldn't judge a book by its cover.

So I am asking you to please tear up the list. Let's ~~treet~~ treat all our customers with kindness and respect and not judge anyone by the color of their skin.

If you have any questions, please call me at 555-281-0482.

Sincerely,
Mia Tang
Assistant Manager
Calivista Motel

I was very proud of our little letter, and so was Hank. Hank said I "hit the issue on the nose," which made me smile. I wrote out ten copies of the letter by hand and went door to door to all the shops on our street.

At most stores, the person inside barely looked at my letter and just put it aside, saying they'd read it later. But then, back at the motel, my phone started ringing.

First the man from the liquor store called up.

"Darn right, you shouldn't judge a customer by the way they look. I mean, heck, if I judged all my customers by the way they look, I'd be out of business. Half my customers can't even walk straight," he said.

I ticked yes next to liquor store in my notebook.

The guy at the convenience store on our street called up next. His voice shook as he spoke.

"I came over from the Philippines seven years ago," said Mr. Abayan. "I'd forgotten what it's like to be judged. I'm ripping the list up right now."

That was a yes for the convenience store.

The Laundromat called up next.

"I never used his silly list anyway. Clothes are clothes. Doesn't matter to me who they're on!" said Mr. Bhagawati.

Yes for Laundromat.

Eight yeses later, it was just down to the other two motels — Lagoon Motel and Topaz Inn. I knew Topaz Inn was out, but Lagoon Motel I still had a shot at. I grabbed my letter and headed over there again.

The manager was an old guy with a raspy voice. He frowned when he saw me.

"What do you want?" he asked.

"Did you read my letter?" I asked.

"Yeah, I read your letter," he said.

"And?"

"I don't know," he said. "Don't get me wrong, kid, I get where you're coming from.

But you and I both know that every time we push that buzzer, we are judging someone based on the way they look. I mean it's not like we're judging them based on their personality or how they eat a fig. We are making a quick, ten-second decision based on what they look like," he said.

"But that's different," I said.

"How's it different?"

"It's not based on their skin color!" I said. "It's based on other things, like are they walking funny, which probably means they're drunk. Are they pounding on the front door, or are they knocking politely?"

"Yeah, but if you think about it —"

I could tell he was one of those people who just loved to argue and we were going to be there all day, so I decided to cut to the chase.

"Look, I've got seven shops who've agreed to not follow the list. Plus us. If you join us, great. If you *don't* join us, I'm going to write a letter to the mayor's office —"

"Gosh darn it, kid," he harrumphed, throwing his arms up. "You and your letters!"

"Are you in, or are you out?" I asked him firmly.

There was a long pause.

"Fine, I'm in," he said finally.

In the end, even Topaz Inn caved too! I told our towel and sheets supplier, who also happened to be their supplier, and was African American. Once he heard about the list, he marched over to the Topaz Inn and threw a fit, threatening to stop selling them supplies unless they cut it out. Without a supplier for their towels and bedding, the Topaz Inn could not operate their business, so they had no choice but to get rid of their list. They apologized and blamed it all on their security guard, whom they promptly fired.

As the security guard crawled by a day after the Topaz let him go, he hollered at me.

"You happy now? You cost me my job, kid!"

I shook my head at him. From the way he was walking, I could tell he'd been drinking.

"We Chinese are supposed to watch out for each other!"

Not if you're being racist!

"My life's ruined because of you."

I turned my back to him, but that just made him more mad.

"Hey! I'm talking to you! Yeah, you. You're sitting there in your nice, air-conditioned office. You think it's all fun and games, don't you? Well, guess what?" he slurred. "It's not! You have *no idea* what it's like for the rest of us. You don't know what it's like to be fired, to have no money and nowhere to go!"

That did it.

"You have no idea what I know!" I yelled back at him. "I've been getting fired since before you could read! I could write a *book* on what it's like to have no money. You know what else I know? That's no excuse to treat other people like dirt!"

The security guard walked away without another word.

CHAPTER 52

There's a saying in Chinese that goes "Never forget how much rice you eat." It's a reminder to stay humble, to stay real. Just because you have an important job doesn't mean you're better than everybody else. You still eat rice, like the rest of us.

Well, that security guard, he definitely forgot. He let the power of his position go straight to his head, and he used it to do horrible things. I wondered if that's what happened to Uncle Zhang's boss too when he took away everybody's passports. At the thought of Uncle Zhang, I felt the stirrings of hope. Did he give the letter to his boss yet?

Uncle Zhang called us from a pay phone two days later.

"You'll never believe it," he said into the phone. "The letter worked! I'm free!"

He told us that when he showed his employer my letter, the guy freaked out. He couldn't believe that Uncle Zhang had found an attorney or at least someone who was able to write good enough English to help him. He got really scared and immediately gave Uncle Zhang back his papers. Not only that, he gave all the other workers back their papers too!

It was the most incredible feeling ever, knowing that something I wrote actually changed someone's life. As my mom and dad and I cheered and congratulated Uncle Zhang, my eyes slid to the closet, where the printout of the essay contest lay.

Maybe, just maybe, I could change our lives too.

"Okay, kids! Get your pencils out," Mrs. Douglas said in class. "We're writing a story again. This time, I want you to write about a small moment in your life."

"A small moment? You mean like a moment that didn't really mean anything?" someone asked.

"Quite the contrary. A moment that meant *everything*," Mrs. Douglas said. "Think of a time when you were ecstatic or terrified, and really zoom in so we know exactly what it felt like."

I stared down at the piece of white paper in front of me. My head was like a train station; so many stories buzzed in and out. I thought about all the things that happened these last few months, all the miracles and heartbreaks. A chorus of voices flooded into me. . . .

Some days, my body was completely inside the Dumpster and all you saw were these two little legs kicking in the air, Uncle Li said.

I kneeled before them, holding their hands as they talked about their Chinese maids and how don't they all steal? Aunt Ling said.

I don't know why she slapped me. All I was said to her was "Hey, baby," said Uncle Fung.

When people look at you, they see a nice, sweet Chinese girl. When they look at me do you know what they see? A criminal, Hank said.

I borrowed the money so she could die knowing her only son was okay out there. That I had made it in America. Uncle Zhang cried.

Even if you're American, you'll still be my sister. You'll always be my sister, wherever you are.

It was this last voice, Shen's voice, that begged, *Let me out!* I wriggled, hoping the feeling would pass. I didn't know how I felt about Mrs. Douglas knowing that much about me.

And yet. I couldn't stop thinking about it, that snowy day in Beijing, how hard it was to step on the plane. How the first thing we did when we arrived was take a shower. I'd never seen a shower before. A private shower, not like those group ones at the bathhouses in China. In China, there was a bathhouse in every neighborhood and everyone went. Sometimes, I'd even see my teacher there. There was awkward, and then there was taking-a-shower-next-to-your-teacher awkward.

"Those days are over! Here we have showers," my dad's friend had bragged when he picked us up from the airport and took us to his apartment. "And you can even open your mouth in the shower and drink the water too! It's clean here. You don't have to boil it."

That first day, I stood in the shower for almost an hour with my mouth open, drenched in bliss, gulping down the deliciousness as the water rained down on me. Afterward, when I looked in the mirror, guilt itched my eyes. Had I just traded my cousin in for a shower? I wondered.

The words gushed out of me. I remembered what Lupe once said about drawing, how it was all in the detail. I closed my eyes and tried to recall every color, sound, and smell. I wrote in such a trance, nearly jumping in my seat when twenty minutes later,

Mrs. Douglas declared there were only two minutes left. I looked down at my river of words. Then I glanced over at Jason next to me.

Panic seized me. The words were so open and exposed. My story looked like a belly button. I immediately wanted to cover it.

Then I remembered something. The itching and wriggling, like a spider was crawling underneath my skin — I'd seen it somewhere before. Where had I seen it? Oh, yes, I remember. It was on Uncle Zhang's face when he told us he was a modern slave. It was on Hank's face too when he finally opened up to me about why nobody wanted to hire him. And look what happened! Their lives changed. If I wanted my life to change, I too needed to get past the itchy, wriggly feeling.

"Okay, guys," Mrs. Douglas said. "Who's finished?"

I took a deep breath and raised my hand.

CHAPTER 53

The moment I handed Mrs. Douglas my story on coming to America was also the moment I decided I *had* to enter the essay competition. I was ready. I could do this.

There was still the tricky issue of the $300 entry fee. I'd been so preoccupied with finding out who stole the missing car, I hadn't been putting out my tip jar. When I went home and fished out the entry form, panic filled my lungs. The deadline was in less than a week! There was no way I could get $300 in tips in that time.

Asking my parents for the money was out. It was the holiday season. You'd think the holiday season would be a busy time for motels, but surprisingly, it's not: Folks would rather stuff themselves inside a tiny closet than have to stay in a motel over the holidays. So I couldn't ask my parents. That left only one option.

My eyes slid down to the bag underneath

my parents' bureau: the lucky pennies.

I know they weren't *my* lucky pennies. They
were *our* lucky pennies. I thought about the
look on my dad's face whenever we found
one of the rare ones — like Christmas
morning. He was so proud of them. I knew
if I told him, he'd never let me sell them.
He was always talking about how much
they'd be worth one day, how they'd appreciate in value over time. He'd never let
me do it. He'd kill himself scraping together
the $300 some other way — probably by
skipping meals and not buying my mom a
Christmas present.

And that I couldn't let him do. Not after
everything they'd been through this year.

So I took the bag of special pennies and
headed over to Hank's. Hank looked down
at the bag.

"Are you sure about this?" Hank asked.

"I'm positive," I said to him.

I explained to him why I needed the
money. Hank nodded and agreed to go
downtown first thing tomorrow before his
shift. I gave him the address of a street in
downtown LA where they traded rare and
valuable coins and stamps. I'd looked it up
in the library.

Before I handed them over, I took one last

look at the pennies. I held them to my cheek and kissed them good-bye.

"I'm going to miss you guys," I whispered.

The next day, Hank returned with $312. I sucked in a breath as he handed me the crisp bills.

"Here you are," he said when he handed me the last of the bills. "Now go win a motel."

"I will!" I said with a grin. Our luck was going to change soon — I could feel it in my bones.

As the honeycomb sun dipped lower into the sky, I sat hunched over at the front desk and wrote my story.

If I Owned a Motel
By Mia Tang

If I owned a motel, I would treat every customer like family. I would bring all guests an extra blanket or a hot-water bottle if they were cold. I would make them a cup of tea if they were having a bad day. And I would get it out of them what happened. Because sometimes terrible things happen, but there's nothing more terrible than not having anybody to tell it to.

Then, after they tell me, I would try to help them. Sometimes, problems seem humongous in your head, but if you tell someone, you'd be surprised what can happen. After we've solved it, we can celebrate together by playing Monopoly after dinner or jumping into the pool together. Life's short and it's important to celebrate the good stuff when it happens.

I would also protect myself and my customers by putting in a security camera, bulletproof glass inside the front office, and a gate so cars can't get stolen. I would charge customers twenty dollars per night for a room but give them a discount if they were a weekly because the weeklies have been living there for a long, long time and that's a lot to pay every day.

If I win your motel, I promise to always treat it with love, kindness, and respect. Your motel won't just be a business to me. It will be home.

Hank came into the front desk just as I was finishing my essay. I handed it to him.

"What do you think?" I asked him when he was done reading.

"It's wonderful," he said. "Just wonderful."

"Is the grammar okay? Do you think I should add anything?" I asked.

"I wouldn't change a thing," Hank said.

His steady eyes looked straight into mine, and years of doubt melted away.

"So this is it, then," I said. "I should just mail it?"

Hank reached down, dug out a card from his back pocket, and handed it to me. It was Lupe's comment card, the one that said *You can't win if you don't play.*

I smiled.

The next day, I mailed in my essay.

CHAPTER 54

At school that day, we had a substitute. Ms. Morgan had big, thick glasses. Whereas Mrs. Douglas was chatty and loud, Ms. Morgan was soft-spoken and cautious.

"It's only my second time teaching," she explained to us.

Some of the other kids, when they heard this, immediately started chatting, talking right over Ms. Morgan even when she clapped her hands two short times and then three long times, which was our class sign to pay attention.

"Really, guys, I must insist you pay attention," Ms. Morgan said quietly, which prompted Jason to cup his ear and ask, "What did you say?"

The other kids thought this was really funny and burst out laughing. Jason was delighted.

For the next half an hour, whenever Ms. Morgan said anything, Jason would blurt out, "Huh? What did you say?"

I kicked Jason repeatedly under my seat to knock it off, but he ignored me.

By lunchtime, Ms. Morgan had lost all control of the class. Now kids were openly raising their hands and saying, "Ms. Mousy, I mean, Ms. Morgan, I have a question," then covering their mouths as they disintegrated into nonstop giggling.

As we filed out one by one for lunch, Ms. Morgan crumbled into her chair.

I went back to the classroom during lunch to grab a copy of my story for the essay contest so that I could show Lupe. As I was about to walk in, though, I heard sniffling.

Ms. Morgan was on the phone. I snuck a peek. Her glasses were on her desk, and she was rubbing her eyes.

"I'm just not cut out for this," she said on the phone. "You don't know what it's like, Wilma. The kids *hate* me."

I immediately froze. I backed up against the wall, next to the open door. I dared not move, afraid that Ms. Morgan might hear me and know that I'd heard. She'd be so embarrassed!

"Maybe I just don't have what it takes to be a real teacher," she said, weeping into the phone.

The lunch bell rang, and Ms. Morgan quickly got off the phone. I waited until some other students filed in first before slipping in too.

As soon as class resumed, Jason started doing the thing with his ear again. "Huh? I really can't hear you. This isn't a church!" he shrieked.

The other kids laughed again. Jason looked around the room, very pleased with himself.

"And you don't *look* like a nun!" he added. Another monstrous wave of laughs. Ms. Morgan looked like she was about to cry.

"Can I talk to you?" I asked Jason.

Jason looked at me like I'd just asked him if he wanted to do the fox-trot.

"Uhhh . . . nooo?" Jason said.

I raised my hand.

"Ms. Morgan, I just remembered. Jason and I need to go to the gym and tell Mr. Henkin, the PE teacher, which kids are absent today," I lied.

"Can't we just call him?" Ms. Morgan asked, picking up the phone.

"No!" I said. "He . . . uh . . . you know, he's out on the field."

"No, he's not," Jason protested. But I

kicked him hard under the seat and he shut up.

Ms. Morgan nodded and said we could go.

When we got outside, I turned to Jason.

"What are you doing?" I asked him.

"What do you mean?"

"Why are you giving Ms. Morgan a hard time?" I said.

"You mean Ms. Mousy?" He laughed.

"It's not funny," I said.

"Seems pretty funny to everyone else."

"Well, I'm not everyone else," I said. "And neither's Ms. Morgan. Did you know I overheard her talking to her friend on the phone and she said she didn't know if she had what it took to be a real teacher? And she was crying."

"So?" Jason snapped, in the tone that reminded me so much of his father, I wanted to throw my hands up and walk away.

But I didn't walk away.

Instead I said very softly, "You don't have to do this."

"Do what?" he asked.

I looked into his eyes.

"You don't have to be your father," I said.

Jason didn't say anything back. He just turned and walked back into the classroom.

He didn't say a word to me the rest of the day.

But he didn't make fun of Ms. Morgan again.

I didn't expect to see Jason again after school, but later that day, he showed up at the motel. Mr. Yao's car roared into the motel around sunset with Jason in the passenger seat. I immediately tossed the baseball cap onto the front desk.

Then I froze.

Two Chinese immigrants had come about an hour ago. I had put them in room 6.

They're here. Chinese visitors were *here.* And so was Mr. Yao.

Frantically, I ran out the back door as Mr. Yao and Jason were getting out of their car.

"Mom! Dad!" I yelled, racing up the stairs.

"Mom, Dad, what?" Mr. Yao asked.

At the sound of Mr. Yao's voice, my parents rushed out of the room. My mom glanced at me and over at room 6.

"Uhhh . . . uhhh . . . we weren't expecting you, Mr. Yao," she said.

Mr. Yao didn't even look up at my mom. He turned his attention instead to the rooms, which, now that it was getting dark outside, were starting to light up, one by one.

"You know, I've been hearing this disgusting little rumor about a motel that's been hiding Chinese immigrants in the rooms," he said.

My dad laughed nervously.

"Where . . . where did you hear that?" he asked. "That's crazy."

"That's what I said. Not only is it crazy but *stupid.* Whoever's stupid enough to do a thing like that is bound to get caught, and when they do, they will never work in this country again. *Never!*"

The entire time he talked, he didn't take his eyes off the rooms. When all the rooms were lit up, he reached into his pocket, pulled out a pen and piece of paper, and started jotting down room numbers. And that's when I knew we were doomed.

Room 6 did not have a registration card.

"Come down," Mr. Yao said to my parents. "Let's take a little walk over to the front desk together, shall we?"

My parents descended the stairs. The sweat stains on my father's shirt stretched and spread.

I lingered behind. If I could just warn the immigrants in room 6, maybe they could slip out or hide. . . .

"Mia!" Mr. Yao yelled.

I jumped. It was the first time Mr. Yao ever

called me by my name.

"Yes?" I asked.

"Stay where I can see you," he hissed. "We're all going to the front desk together, and if the numbers on my list don't match the registration cards, there will be hell to pay!"

In the front office, Mr. Yao picked up the stack of registration cards and started flinging them onto the table one by one as he cross-referenced them with his list. When at last he came to room 6 and saw there were no registration cards, he pounded the table with his hand.

"Are you hiding immigrants in my motel?" he screamed at my dad. "Is that what you're doing? Look at me when I'm talking to you!"

My dad lifted his eyes inch by inch.

"No, sir," my dad denied.

"Don't lie to me! I was born at night but not last night."

Mr. Yao was standing so close to him, his angry words fell like spittle on my dad.

"I'm going to give you one last chance to tell me just who the hell is in room six," he said in a low voice.

"I don't know, sir," my dad said.

"You don't *know*?" Mr. Yao asked. "Are

you saying some people just snuck in and started sleeping there? Because if that's the case, I will call the cops right now."

His threat cut into us like glass. My mom and I looked at each other. Mr. Yao was making my dad choose between his job and his friends. And we both knew which my dad would choose. There was no way my dad would throw the people in room 6 under the bus. Not in a million years. As he opened his mouth to confess, I jumped in.

"You must have gotten the number wrong. There's no one in there," I said.

"We'll just see about that," Mr. Yao growled.

As he lifted the front desk divider to go outside, a car pulled into the motel. Mr. Yao stopped for a minute to see who it was. The girl with the jeans stepped out of the car. She'd come back with her mom.

My blood curdled when I saw her. I looked down at my jeans — her jeans — as the girl and her mom stepped into the front office.

"Mother, look!" She pointed at my jeans. "*Those* are mine. You *stole* my jeans!"

All around me, eyes narrowed — her eyes, Mr. Yao's eyes, her mother's eyes. I looked down at my jeans and up at her. I didn't know what to do. I didn't know what to say.

So I lied.

"These are mine," I said.

Mr. Yao's mouth curled into a tight smile as he put his stack of registration cards down and turned his full attention to the girl. Sweat dripped down my spine, even as the front office air conditioner blasted on me.

"Is it true? Did you steal this girl's pants?" Mr. Yao asked, not even looking at me.

I squirmed in the jeans, the hard fabric digging into my flesh.

"No . . . I . . ." I struggled to speak. My throat felt like sand. "I didn't. I don't steal, I swear."

"Liar!" the girl said.

Jason looked away. I followed his gaze out the window to my parents, who had tiptoed out of the back and were now standing in front of room 6. I quickly looked over at Mr. Yao, but he was too busy gawking at me like I was a criminal to notice where my parents had gone.

"Of course you stole them," Mr. Yao said. "You're a thief. That's probably what you were doing at Macy's too when my wife saw you!"

"It was not!"

I glared at him. I resented the way he looked at me, like he knew me so well, when in fact he knew *nothing* about me.

"I don't steal!" I repeated.

"You're saying these are *your* jeans?"

"Yes," I insisted, with as much conviction as I could muster.

The girl pointed at the jeans.

"Show us the label then," she said. She turned to Mr. Yao and added, "My name's written in permanent marker on the label."

Ugh! I knew I should have cut off the label.

"Do it or I'll do it," Mr. Yao commanded. He took a step toward me. Before he could dig his gross fingers into my jeans, I reached behind, squeezed my eyes shut and pulled out the label.

There, in all bold, shouty caps was the name POLLY written in permanent marker.

"Take them off," Mr. Yao barked at me. "NOW."

Polly smirked. She was clearly enjoying this. Mr. Yao pointed to the manager's quarters.

"Go," he said.

I limped into my room and quietly closed the door.

The jeans felt hot to my touch. I peeled them off like bark, stomping on them on the cold floor in my socks. Tears pooled at the base of my eyes as I stared at the jeans — hours ago, my friend, my pride — and now my shame.

I got out my ugly floral pants and put them back on. Fear pressed me forward — the fear that if I didn't emerge from my room, they'd come barging in.

"Here," I said, handing the jeans back to the girl.

I didn't apologize, nor did I cry.

I refused to give Mr. Yao the satisfaction.

CHAPTER 55

"I thought the whole point of having customers fill in their address was so you could mail them their stuff back in case they left it behind," Mr. Yao said after the girl and her mom left. "Wasn't that *your* idea?"

I couldn't speak. The humiliation had burned a hole in my tongue. I vowed never to talk to him again.

My parents slipped back in through the back door and joined us.

"Where'd you guys go?" Mr. Yao asked. "You guys missed the whole thing!"

In all his excitement over the jeans, he had completely forgotten about the immigrants in room 6. I looked up at my mom and could tell from her face that they were safe. My mom would never know the price I paid for their safety.

Jason knew. The whole time his dad was interrogating me, he had been looking out the window. He saw my parents knock on room 6's door. He saw them sneak the immigrants out of their rooms and out the back. He saw the whole thing.

But he never said anything.

Dear Jason,
    Thank you for not saying anything to your dad. I don't know why but you didn't. Maybe you're not so bad after all.

Your ~~friend~~ classmate,
Mia

I stared at the last part. *Maybe you're not so bad after all.*

My grandmother used to say that people don't change. Our heart is like a rubber band. It might stretch a little, but eventually it snaps right back.

I'm not sure if I believed that. Part of me did. We were talking about Jason here, the same kid who took my pencil and licked it. The other part of me, though . . . wondered.

There used to be a time when I let my cousins walk all over me. They were all boys, and I was the only girl, and in China, girls are kind of like spare tires. It's nice if you have one, but they're not *important.* Even my grandmother, whom I loved and missed so much, believed this. She believed it like she believed the sky was blue. Like it was a fact. Girls were just not as useful as boys.

She never came out and said this, of course. But she'd have little ways of showing it, like always putting the best dishes in front of my cousins at family dinners and not me. She'd pat their heads and tell them to eat up before the dish got cold. And I'd watch as they snatched and grabbed the food with their greedy chopsticks until there were hardly any more pieces of chicken left for me, only burnt onions.

One day, I picked up my chopsticks and started grabbing back. I snagged chicken, shrimp, whatever I could pick up with my chopsticks and hoarded it all in my mouth.

"Hey!" Shen complained. "Not fair!"

We weren't close then, and I narrowed my eyes at him.

As I picked up my chopsticks to reach for more food, Shen blocked my chopsticks with his. Our chopsticks collided like swords. The two of us held them in position, neither willing to back down.

It went on like this the next night, and the night after that. Eventually, our chopsticks war got so bad, my grandmother had to use her own chopsticks to draw a "line" in the food and declare one side mine and the other side Shen's.

From then on, every dish had a line. I remember countless birthdays, Chinese New Year — everything had a line.

Then one day I looked down and the line was gone. My grandmother had forgotten to draw it. I waited for Shen to take the first piece of chicken, and he waited for me. Neither of us grabbed. Neither of us hoarded. Somehow, we'd gone from food enemies to friends. Neither of us knew when it had happened. We just knew we no longer needed the line.

I thought about that and how maybe people do change, as I thought about Jason.

I didn't end up giving the letter to Jason. I was going to, but for some reason, I just didn't. You know how sometimes you raise your hand, but when the teacher finally calls on you, you pretend you were only tucking your hair? It was kind of like that.

As the first of the spring flowers bloomed, I tried to forget the painful memory of the jeans. It helped that I had Hank and Lupe to distract me. And the mailman. Every time he came, I thought about the contest. I thought, *This is it. Today's the day my life's going to change!*

But the letter from Vermont did not arrive. Other unexpected news did arrive, though, which completely shook up our world: Mr. Yao was selling the motel.

My parents' faces turned white. The temperature in the room plummeted as Mr. Yao told them the news.

A real estate deal for him in Nevada had gone bad, and he needed a cash injection.

"So what does that mean for us?" my parents asked him.

"*You?*" Mr. Yao asked. He snorted, like we hadn't occurred to him at all. Then he shrugged. "Depends on what the new owner wants to do with you."

He said it like we were inventory — freely disposable, along with the washer and dryer.

Lupe told me not to worry. Motels weren't like houses. They took ages to sell.

"There's a whole inspection process and everything," she said. "I'm sure you guys are going to be out of here before Mr. Yao even finds a buyer. Have you told your parents about the essay contest yet?"

"No . . ." I said.

I didn't know what it was about me and secrets. Once I had one, I just couldn't let it go. I would feed it and snuggle it, and it would grow and grow inside me until it took on a life all its own! So no, I hadn't told my parents. I'd been too busy imagining the look of surprise on their face to actually surprise them.

"They're going to *freak* when you win!" Lupe said with a smile.

My parents did freak, but not over my winning the contest. They were freaking out over who the new motel owner was going to be.

"Oh God, what if he hates Chinese people?" my mother asked, biting down on her nail.

"Or if he wants to run it himself?" my father said.

"Should we look for another job?" my mom asked. "What should we do?"

My parents paced the living room, fretting and panicking, while I sat quietly in the corner. That was the problem with keeping a secret — you are all alone, on your own little island.

"Have you ever thought about how nice it would be if we owned the motel?" I asked.

I just kind of threw it out there.

My dad laughed.

"That would be nice," he said.

He looked into the distance and let himself imagine . . . for a second.

"We wouldn't have to work every single

day. We can take Sundays off. Together, as a family!"

"We could all go swimming!" my mom added. "I'd love to jump in that pool!"

"Me too!" I said.

"I'd love to get some *sleep,*" my dad said. "If we owned the motel, I could put up a sign that says *Sorry, I'm sleeping. Come back in the morning.*"

A smile played at his lips as he pictured how extraordinary life would be if he could sleep through the night.

Then his smile faded and reality set in.

"Maybe in another life," he said, picking up his broom.

I shook my head.

"No, Dad, not in another life," I said. "In this life."

Our eyes locked.

A second passed, and then another.

And then I whispered my secret.

CHAPTER 56

They didn't say a word at first. I thought perhaps they were too shocked. Sometimes when I'm too shocked, I can't speak either. That's why I write things down, and even then, sometimes I can't bring myself to deliver them. Like my thank-you letter to Jason, which was just sitting there at the bottom of my backpack.

I thought maybe my parents were just taking their time too. Taking their time to find the right words. But then I looked up and saw my mother's disappointment.

"You're not going to win," she said.

Her voice was certain, positive. She looked right at me, her eyes a mixture of pain and sadness, but not sad like I'm-sad-you're-not-going-to-win, sad like I'm-sad-you-actually-thought-you-could-win.

I wanted to grab her and shake her. "You're wrong, Mom. I'm not a bike. You'll see," I yelled.

My mom put her hands on my arms.

"No, honey!" she said. "I mean those sweepstakes are all *rigged*!"

The news slapped me across the face. For a second, I was fully blind. And then I flat-out denied it.

"It's not rigged!"

"No, of course not," my dad jumped in.

"But just think about it. Why would they just give away a motel like that?" my mother asked.

"Because they're old," I said. "They don't care about the money. They're doing it out of the goodness of their heart!"

"Have you ever seen anybody in this country do something out of the goodness of their heart?"

"The doctor who fixed you up — remember him?"

My mother's face softened. She didn't talk about the contest being rigged after that. Still, the doubt lingered with me. What if she was right?

CHAPTER 57

Mr. Yao came over the next day, poring over the numbers and figures in the big ledger with an intensity I'd never seen before. He took over the entire front desk, making calls and pounding so madly on the calculator, I thought it might break. I didn't really want to be in the same room with him, after what happened with the jeans, but I stayed behind so I could put the blue baseball cap on the table.

Mr. Yao looked up from the ledger. He pointed at the blue baseball cap.

"That used to be the old manager's," he said.

I didn't say anything. I didn't feel like talking to Mr. Yao, and especially not about the hat.

"His name was Ye Fei, but he called himself Jerry," he continued. He picked the hat up and chuckled to himself. "I remember when he got this hat. He didn't even know what the Yankees were!"

"So why'd he get it?" I wondered out loud, instantly frowning because I'd broken my vow never to talk to Mr. Yao again. *Darn.*

"He liked the way the Y looked. His name starts with Y," he said. Mr. Yao put the cap back on the desk and looked into the distance. "He was a good guy, that Ye. Very hard worker."

Wait, what?? Had I heard that right?

"The two before him, totally useless. Incompetent doesn't even cut it. They couldn't do a single thing without calling me," he said, shaking his head.

"How many managers have you had?" I asked him.

"Oh, I don't know, I don't count these things."

And . . . we were back. *These things.*

"But he was a good one, that Ye."

I wondered for a second how Mr. Yao would talk about us after we left for Vermont. How would he take the news?

"Sooner or later, they all leave," Mr. Yao answered with a sigh, as if he had read my thoughts.

Maybe if he was nicer to them, they wouldn't leave, I thought. As I gazed at Mr. Yao, his face hardened by all the years and managers who had come and gone, I wondered what young Mr. Yao was like when he first started out. Was he less of a jerk, or the same? I wished I could ask him.

The phone disrupted my thoughts. Mr. Yao grabbed it and in an instant he was back to his usual no-nonsense, you're-only-as-good-as-your-last-envelope self.

"Bobby. No, listen, I'll get you the money —" he said into the phone, waving me away to give him some privacy.

I went into my room and replayed what Mr. Yao said about the old manager in my head. A part of me hoped he would say good things about us after we left. Even if he never said them to us.

The next week, the letter I'd been waiting for arrived. I held it in my trembling hands, staring and staring at the words *Vermont Motel Giveaway Committee,* terrified of what it might contain.

"Hank!" I shouted. "It's here!"

As the weeklies and my parents piled into the manager's quarters, Hank stood up and cleared his throat.

"Everyone! I think that we can all agree that little Mia here has changed our lives, each and every one of us in this room," Hank said.

Heads nodded. "Hear, hear," Billy Bob said.

Mrs. Q reached over and gave my hand a squeeze.

"Well, now it's her turn. Today, our girl's life is going to change. And it's *about* time, I say!" Hank exclaimed.

"Woooo!" Fred cheered.

Hank took his glass of cream soda and held it up. "To Mia!"

Everyone held up their glasses.

"To Mia!" the room boomed.

I looked around the room, the corners of my eyes wet with gratitude. Love welled inside me as I smiled back at the weeklies. Here we were, strangers from all corners of the world, blown to the Calivista by the winds of life, only to find each other and reemerge as a new family.

"Thank you guys so much," I said.

I thought about how much I was going to miss the weeklies in Vermont, especially Hank. A lump formed in my throat.

Hank pointed at the envelope in my hand. "May I do the honor?" he asked me.

I nodded.

He took the envelope from me.

"This is it, people." Hank rubbed his hands together.

We all held our breaths as Hank opened

the envelope. My heart raced so hard, I thought it might come flying out.

As Hank unfolded the letter, my mother put her fist to her teeth, her knuckles the color of porcelain. My father's knees were on the floor, his hands folded together, eyes on the ceiling.

" 'Thank you for applying for the Vermont Motel giveaway,' " Hank read. " 'We've read every single entry over very carefully, and we regret to inform you —' "

Hank's smile vanished.

"What — what is it?" I asked.

Hank put the letter down and I knew.

CHAPTER 58

We sat in silence, the hot tears pooling in my eyes, Billy Bob's hands balling into fists, and Mrs. Q shaking her head, blinking hard, blowing her nose into a tissue like someone had died. Because in a way, that's what it felt like. Our dream had died.

"This is bull!" Hank yelled. He looked madder than I'd ever seen him before, madder even than when he threw that drunk guy out.

"It's okay," I said softly.

"No, it's not okay!" he bellowed. He got up and walked across the room. "How could they do this?"

"Maybe what I wrote just wasn't . . ." The lump in my throat become a boulder. "Just wasn't good."

They slithered in like eels — *You're a bike. The other kids are cars. You'll never be as good as the white kids in their language.* I tried to stop it, but it was no use. Doubt came in through every pore.

Hank shook his head.

"You know what? I'll bet the whole thing's a scam," Hank said. "They're probably not even giving away a motel. They just wanted the money! Probably thought three hundred dollars is nothing to people. They didn't know you sold your lucky pennies."

My dad's face plunged.

"You . . . you sold the lucky pennies?" he asked. He looked away immediately, but there was a second. A second in which I saw into him crystal clear. I saw his hope fade away.

"We'll help you find new ones," Hank said, looking around at the other weeklies. "We'll all look, won't we?"

The weeklies instantly started digging into their pockets for loose change.

"No. It's fine," my dad said. "I'm fine."

Later that night, the weeklies went back to their rooms, and I sat with an emptiness that was almost unbearable. I went out the back to look for my dad. I found him sitting by himself in the laundry room.

"Hey, Dad," I said.

He looked up at me, his eyes pink and moist, like he'd been crying. "Hey, sweetheart," he said. He quickly dabbed his eyes with the towels.

"I'm sorry I sold our lucky pennies," I said to him. I told myself I wasn't going to cry, but the tears came anyway. My father pulled me into his arms.

"Hey, no, it's okay. You win some and you lose some," he said, kissing the top of my head.

"But I always lose some."

My dad looked down at me and wiped a tear away too.

"That's not true," he said. "Because of you, Uncle Zhang's now free. Hank has a new job. I'd call that a win."

"But I really wanted to win for *us* this time," I muttered.

My dad rocked me in his arms.

"I know you did, sweetheart," he said, his voice shaking. "I know you did."

CHAPTER 59

"So that's it, I'm not going," I told Lupe at school the next day.

"I can't believe this!" she said. "Did they say who won?"

I shook my head.

"I bet it was their cousin or their son or something stupid like that," she said. "It couldn't have been your essay. I read your essay — it was so good."

It felt good to hear her say that, although a part of me still wasn't sure.

We were sitting on the grass in PE, way out in left field, avoiding the ball and any chance of injury as usual. Lupe picked a blade of grass and twirled it around her finger.

"You know, I'm kind of glad you're not going," she said.

"So you don't have to stay with Jason all by yourself?" I asked, squinting at her in the sun.

"So I don't have to stay on the roller coaster all by myself," she whispered.

It occurred to me at that moment what it would have been like for Lupe if I had left. I always thought I was the one who needed her, that I was the barnacle to her whale. But it wasn't one way. We needed each other, me and Lupe. She had been trying to tell me this all along, but it never really hit me until now.

"Well, you don't have to worry," I said. "I'm not going anywhere."

Lupe smiled at me.

"I'll be on the roller coaster for a long, long time," I said.

Lupe shook her head.

"Nope, you're not. You're getting off," she said. "We're both getting off. Together."

She put her hand on top of mine, and I looked down at our two hands on the grass.

Later that day, after we had filed back into class, Mrs. Douglas turned to us and clapped our signal. As everyone sat up in their seats and listened up, she turned to me.

"Mia, will you please come up to the front of the class?" Mrs. Douglas asked.

I glanced worriedly at Lupe as I got up and walked over.

"Now, class, you all remember the stories I asked you to write a while back about a small moment in your life?" Mrs. Douglas asked.

My heart jumped to my throat.

"Mia here wrote about what it was like to come to America on an airplane," she said. "Anyway, the other fifth-grade teachers and I got together, and we read everyone's story, and we all agree that Mia's story . . ."

She paused for what felt like an eternity. I squeezed my eyes shut.

". . . is absolutely *wonderful*."

My jaw dropped.

Mrs. Douglas handed me my story. "Mia, will you please read your story to the rest of the class?"

I blinked at Mrs. Douglas, waiting for her to say, *Oh, wait, there's been a mistake.* Was this going to be like the chocolate notebook again? I told myself, *Don't. Do* not *feel warm and fuzzy. Not yet.*

But then I snuck a peek down at my paper. There were red marks all over it, just like the last time, and lots and lots of exclamation marks. But they didn't scream *BAD GRAMMAR!!* in shouty caps. They said things like *Moved me to tears!!* and *Oh, Mia! This is incredible!!*

"Go on," Mrs. Douglas said. "Read your

story to the class."

"Right now?" I asked.

Mrs. Douglas nodded.

With trembling hands, I took it from her and slowly began to read.

As I read, my voice wavered. My throat was prickly, my lips dry. Still, I pushed forward in my tiny voice.

When I finished reading, the whole room was silent. Everyone's eyes were on me. I stood so still, if a breeze swept through the classroom, I would have fallen.

And then, amid the deafening silence, I heard a sound. The sound of clapping. I looked up to see Lupe clapping. A few kids joined her, and soon, almost everyone in the room was clapping. Even Jason Yao!

I felt my throat pinch with emotion.

"That was beautiful," Mrs. Douglas said.

I looked up at the swelling pride in her face and instantly forgave her for giving away my sparkly pencil.

"Thank you, Mrs. Douglas," I said, and started going back to my seat.

"Wait," Mrs. Douglas said. "I have something for you."

She reached inside her desk and pulled out a small piece of paper, which she handed to me. I peered at the words *Pizza*

Hut written on it.

"Two free pizzas at Pizza Hut, for you and a friend," she said.

I looked up at Mrs. Douglas. I looked into her eyes, *Are you sure? Are you sure there hasn't been a mistake?* When enough time passed and I was finally sure she wasn't going to take it away, I looked over at Lupe. Her eyes sparkled with excitement.

CHAPTER 60

"Mom!" I raced up the stairs two at a time.

My parents were in the middle of cleaning room 22. My mother was holding Windex in one hand and Lysol in the other.

"Mom! Dad! Guess what? I won a writing contest at school!" I exclaimed.

"Are you serious?" my mom asked. "When did this happen?"

"Today," I said, handing her my coupon to Pizza Hut.

My dad beamed. He put the vacuum cleaner down, took me into his arms, and spun me around.

"What'd I tell you? You win some and you lose some!" he exclaimed.

I grinned.

"Lupe's coming over," I said to my mom. "Will you take us to Pizza Hut?"

"Will I ever!" my mom said, tossing her Lysol and Windex to the side.

I laughed.

Ever since I could remember, my mom had been asking my dad to take her out to eat, but of course, we could never afford it. And now we could finally go. We didn't even need to carry a fake shopping bag!

The pizza at Pizza Hut was bubbling hot. My mouth watered before I even tasted it, just from the smell wafting toward us from the kitchen. Lupe dug into hers, smiling as she devoured the cheese.

"This is *so* good," Lupe said.

I put a slice onto my mom's plate. She took a bite and purred. It was almost enough just watching the two of them, I was so happy. I looked around the room, thinking of all the times I'd walked by this place, peering through the windows, wondering what it was like to sit in one of the booths.

"Mia! You gotta taste this!" My mom pointed to my slice.

I took a bite and felt the soft dough melt in my mouth. I'd had pizza before at school but not like this. I closed my eyes, savoring every morsel of cheese and pepperoni. It was heavenly.

My mother looked at me and said, "I'm so proud of you."

"Not bad for a bicycle, right?" I asked with a grin. I couldn't resist.

My mom put the pizza down and turned to me.

"You're not a bicycle," she said. "The truth is, *I'm* the bicycle."

"Mom, you're not —"

"Yes, I am. You see how my English is. My English is terrible."

I thought about the stupid woman who made fun of my mom's pronunciation. "So you say *eggplant eggplan'*. Who cares?"

My mom shook her head. "It's not only that. It's . . . everything." She looked down at the ground, then back up at me. "Math I could help you with, but, Mia, I cannot help you with English!"

I finally understood why my mother had been saying all these things. She didn't want to hurt me. She wanted to help me. And she couldn't with English. That's why she was constantly pushing me to do math. I wanted to say to her, *Mom, have faith in me. I can do it on my own. I figured the front desk out on my own, didn't I?*

"Don't worry, Mom," I said to her. "You don't have to always help me. I can do it."

My mom didn't say anything for a long time. Then she smiled.

"Clearly you can," she said.

That afternoon, as we inhaled slice after

slice of deliciousness, my mom asked Lupe about her family in Mexico.

"We left when I was very little, and I don't get to see them very often," Lupe said.

"Why don't you guys go back and visit? I mean, since it's so close," I said. I would go back every day if China were right there.

Lupe shrugged.

"My mom says every time we go, we have to buy so many presents for everyone. I have eleven cousins — and that's just on my mom's side," Lupe said. "On my dad's side I have, let's see . . ."

Lupe counted on her fingers.

"Seven!" she announced.

"You must miss them so much," my mom said, glancing at me.

"Sometimes," she said. "But they all think America's this super-rich place where everyone just plays golf all day and drives around in a Cadillac."

My mother laughed.

"It's the same with my siblings," my mom said. "I think they get that from the movies."

Lupe sighed.

"I wish there was a movie that told them what it's really like," Lupe said.

My mom shook her head.

"No way," my mom said. "That would be

so embarrassing."

Lupe reached for another slice.

"This is really nice, by the way," Lupe said, looking at me. "Thanks for inviting me."

I smiled back at her. There was nobody in the world I'd rather share this with . . . well, except . . .

"Hey, should we save some for Dad?" I asked.

I bet he'd never tasted anything like this before. Real pizza, not the frozen kind from the grocery store. Against our stomachs' loud protests, I put my slice down and so did my mother. She raised her hand for a to-go box.

Back at the motel, we found my dad in the kitchen making himself some rice with cabbage.

"Forget the cabbage," my mom said with a smile as she handed him the pizza box. "Look what your daughter brought you."

My dad huffed and puffed about how we didn't have to do that, but I could tell he was secretly glad we did.

As he bit into the pizza, he closed his eyes and moaned.

CHAPTER 61

The kind people at Pizza Hut let me keep my coupon as a souvenir. Carefully, I taped it up next to the front desk so I could look at it every day while I worked.

I wished I could tell my cousin Shen about it. The whole time Lupe was talking about her cousins in Mexico, I was thinking about Shen. There was this restaurant that Shen and I would always walk by on our way to school. It was a fancy Western restaurant, the only one in town, and naturally, it was way too expensive. Every time we walked by it, Shen and I would talk about what it'd be like to one day go in there when we grew up and order whatever we want. If Shen knew that today I'd gone to Pizza Hut — and for free too! — he'd be so proud of me. I smiled at the thought.

I pulled out a piece of paper and started writing him a letter. If my mom didn't want to tell his mom anything about her, fine, but I just *had* to tell Shen.

It'd been a while since I last wrote — the last letter was before we started working for Mr. Yao. I wrote quickly, scribbling away about Lupe and Hank and Mr. Yao. I wrote about the car theft and the crazy security guard and freeing Uncle Zhang. I wrote about school and Jason, who wasn't *quite* so bad anymore, even though he still had my pencil. I told him about the essay contest and how I didn't win, but that Lupe and I were going to figure out another way to get off the roller coaster together. Finally, I told him about Mrs. Douglas and my writing, how it'd gone from twelve exclamation marks bad to four exclamation marks good!

I even drew a picture of the Pizza Hut coupon so he could see for himself. In my neatest handwriting, I copied down all the words on the coupon, including the little expiration date at the bottom so he would know exactly what it looked like.

I was nearly done when the mailman came.

"Can you just wait a second?" I begged the mailman. "I want to mail this letter to my cousin in China and I just need to get the address from my parents. It'll just take a second."

"Did you say China?" he asked. He poked

340

around in his big sack of letters and pro-
duced an envelope. "Looks like you just got
something from there today!"

I peered at the letter in his hands. I
couldn't believe my eyes when I saw the ad-
dressee. It was from Shen!

"Thank you so much!" I told the mailman. I was so excited, I forgot all about
mailing my own letter to Shen, and tore
open his letter to me.

The mailman chuckled as he left.

It was a very long letter — five pages long,
to be exact. It was extremely detailed, and
Shen even separated it into sections — there
was a section on school, a section on neighborhood, and a section on our family. Typical him — he was always super organized.

I raced through the letter, gulping it down
as quickly as I could. I giggled at Shen's
description of his new teacher, Mr. Wang,
and how he couldn't sneeze without farting
at the same time. He told me all about the
new kids at his school, many of whom were
from the outskirts of the city. The entire
neighborhood was changing; all throughout
the city, people were starting to buy up
property. The government was tearing down
the old brick buildings to make room for
new high-rises.

When I got to the section on family,

though, my eyes did a double take.

We recently moved to an apartment by the river because it's bigger. After you guys left, my dad was made head of department at his job. Long story short, the job came with a much bigger apartment. I no longer have to share with my parents — now I have my own room!

Oh, and we also got a car. Nothing like what you guys have in America, I'm sure, but it's pretty great. Last weekend, we went to Beijing and walked around the Great Wall. We had lunch at a brand-new Peking duck restaurant. It was really fancy. Do they have Peking duck in America?

Over and over, I read the words. New apartment. Own room. Car.

I looked down at my own letter on the table, at my handwriting, which a minute ago looked neat and now looked puny. Slowly, I reread my words, how I'd gone on and on about the poor roller coaster and my pencil, my excitement of finally going to an American restaurant, how my stomach growled when I made myself put the pizza back so I could save some for my dad. The more I read, the more my fingers stiffened.

Suddenly, I didn't feel like sending my

letter anymore.

With my hands heavy as rocks, I took my letter and Shen's letter and walked over to my closet. I stuffed them both way in the back, together with my C-minus story and the rejection letter from the essay contest.

Was it true — was Shen rich now? The wild thought bounced around in my head as I tossed and turned. My lips formed around the word. *Rich . . . rich . . .*

It was like a passcode to a different galaxy. And now Shen was part of the galaxy and I wasn't. Could it be that while our life had gotten so hard, his life had gotten so much easier?

The thought was so painful to bear, I couldn't stand it. I rushed to lick my wounds.

Shen may have his own room now, but I was pretty sure he still didn't have a bathroom with a shower. He still had to go to the neighborhood bathhouse. And his dad may have gotten a good job, but they'd still never flown in an airplane and never stayed in a hotel before.

With every *never,* I felt my panic subside.

Later, when I could finally breathe again, guilt cut into me like the harsh fluorescent front office lights. How could I feel this way about my own cousin? He was family. If he was doing well, I should be happy for him. I should be proud of him, because after all, if his family was rich now, didn't that mean . . .

I sat up in bed.

"MOM!!!!"

CHAPTER 62

My parents thought it was a joke.

"You want *your aunt* to buy the Calivista?" They burst out laughing.

"Why not?" I asked. I showed them Shen's letter, the part about how everyone in the city was starting to buy up property.

"They're not going to buy a motel," my dad said.

"Fine, they don't have to buy it, but they can lend us the money. *We* can buy it! And we could run it with Lupe and her family," I said.

"They don't have that kind of money!" my dad said. "If they did, they wouldn't be in China."

"Well, it doesn't hurt to ask," I said.

"No way!" My mom screwed up her face. "I'm not going to ask my sister for money!"

Sometimes when my parents got like this, I really wanted to spray them with all-purpose cleaner. "Don't you guys want to get off the roller coaster?" I asked. "Mr. Yao wants to sell the motel. I heard him on the phone — he's desperate! Aunt Juli has money now. *We* could buy the motel! Don't you see what a huge opportunity this is?"

No, my mom didn't see.

"I see your head's in the clouds, is what I see," my mom said flatly.

Hank found me later that afternoon sitting at the back of the stairs.

"Why so blue?" he asked, taking a seat.

I shrugged.

"You still thinking about your lucky pennies?"

I shook my head. I wasn't thinking about *those* lucky pennies. I was thinking about this one, the humongous penny staring us in the face. It was called family and my parents refused to pick it up!

When I told Hank, he got up, patted my head, and said, "Don't worry. Leave it to me."

He walked up to where my parents' maid cart was, and I followed him. My parents were in room 13 cleaning. Hank walked in and sat down on the bed.

"You know, it's a funny thing, pride," Hank said to my parents. "It's stopped me many times in my life."

Hank glanced at me and added, "And I'm not just talking about my reference letter."

My mom put her broom down and wiped the sweat off her forehead. She sat down on the bed next to Hank.

Hank took a deep breath and gazed outside, in the general direction of the pool.

"I'm talking about when I was young." He sighed. "When I was six, I wanted to be a swimmer. I just loved watching swimming on TV. There wasn't a pool in my neighborhood, so I would walk five miles to the Y over in the next town to go swimming. And I got pretty good. In high school, I tried out for the swim team. And you know what? I made it too. I made it onto the team."

I smiled. "So then what happened?" I asked.

Hank grimaced. He told us about the other kids on the team and how they kept making fun of him.

"They kept saying stuff like 'The basketball court's that way' and 'Why're you putting on sunscreen? You don't need sunscreen!' Stuff like that." He shook his head.

I reached over and put my hand over his.

"I thought I would show them in the water, you know, show them how fast I was. That'll shut them up. But the day of the big meet came and guess what?"

"What?" I asked.

"I was dead last. It wasn't even close. So you know what I did?"

"What?"

"I quit. Just walked on out and never came back," he said.

"Good for you," my mom said. "You're better off without them!"

"See, that's what I used to think, but now you know what I think? I think if it were Mia, she wouldn't have quit. She wouldn't have let those punks take away her dream. She would have worked hard and gotten better. So what if you lose the first race, you get back in there and keep swimming. And you know something? She would have been right."

I thought back to all the times Hank walked by the pool, how he always stopped and stared at it, his mind a million miles away.

Hank turned back to my parents.

"The point I'm trying to make is you can't let a useless thing like pride get in the way of your dreams," Hank said. "That's what I realized this year." Hank pointed at me. "Now, you've got a very special little girl here. You owe it to her to swallow your pride," he said. "I've been around long enough to know there aren't many chances in life for our lot to change our luck. And this is it. You're staring at it. Yao's dying to sell the motel."

"But it's not that simple. I've been *lying* to my sisters about how great our life here is," my mom confessed.

"So tell them the truth! No skin off your back," Hank said.

My mom looked hesitantly at my dad.

"Hank's got a point," my dad said.

"Please, Mom," I added.

My mother peered into my eyes. Hesitation melted into resolve. Slowly, she stretched out her hand.

"Give me the phone," my mom said.

We all crowded around my mother as she picked up the phone in the room and dialed international for my aunt, a number she knew by heart yet never used.

My father looked at his watch.

"What time is it over there?" he wondered. "Probably nine, ten, in the morning?"

We waited and waited while it rang. Finally, on the fifth ring, my aunt picked up.

"Juli?" my mother said in her rapid-fire Chinese. "It's Ying!"

My mother's face lit up when she heard

her sister's voice. I guess all the lies in the world couldn't pull two sisters apart.

"We're doing great," my mom said. "Everything's fine. Just terrific."

Uh-oh. I could feel her Macy's voice coming on.

"Listen, the reason I called is I have an opportunity for you," my mom said. My mom glanced hesitantly at my dad who nodded. *Go on.* "How would you like to invest in some American property?"

A pause.

"Yeah, I said American property," my mother repeated. "Not just any property — a motel! See, the owner of our motel, Mr. Yao, is selling his motel. And I just thought —"

I could hear my aunt's animated voice on the other line, but I couldn't make out what she was saying.

"No, you wouldn't have to run it. We could run it for you. It's a real cash cow this motel," my mom said. "A wonderful opportunity."

My mom's face fell.

"I see."

I could tell from the look on my mom's face my aunt wasn't going for it.

My mom held her hand over the receiver and whispered to us, "She says they're saving up to buy an apartment in Beijing for Shen."

An apartment for Shen? Shen's only ten!

"No, of course I understand. But listen, you don't have to put in a lot. You could ask Qin, Lan, Biming. You could ask the whole neighborhood! Everybody could each put in a little."

Qin, Lan, and Biming were my mom's other siblings.

My mom frowned.

"Oh. They want to buy an apartment in Beijing too, huh," she said.

My mom shifted her weight from one foot to the other. I could tell she was ready to give up and I poked her. *No.* My mom looked over at us.

Tell her, my dad mouthed.

"Okay, listen," she sighed into the phone. "The truth is . . . we're really struggling here."

Slowly, my mom put aside her Macy's voice and told my aunt the truth.

"So I'm asking," my mom said at last, her voice shaking. "Will you help us, Sis?"

There was a long pause at the other end of the line during which my mom, Hank, and I all held our breaths.

As my aunt delivered her verdict, my mom sank onto the bed.

CHAPTER 63

My mother was inconsolable that night. She couldn't believe that her sister would rather buy a fancy penthouse in Beijing than help her own sibling. As she buried her head into her pillow, my father tried his best to comfort her.

"I can't believe she said no," my mom said to my dad.

I couldn't either. Never in a million years did I think my aunt would say no, not after my mom told her what we were going through. I guess a lot had changed since we left — not just the neighborhood, but the people too. They were probably splitting the bill now.

"It's okay," my dad said. "We tried. You heard what Hank said, it's no skin off our back."

"It *is*," my mom cried. "It's the skin and the hair and everything!" I bit my lip as I listened from my bed. "Now we'll just be employees for the rest of our lives, working for one bastard after another."

"Not everyone can lead, Ying," my dad said. "Some people are just destined to be followers."

As my father started going on about our fate again, I threw my head back down onto the pillow. I didn't believe we were destined to be followers. I didn't believe we were just supposed to stay on the roller coaster forever.

I thought about all the people I'd met this year and how we all deserved better — Lupe, Hank, the other weeklies, and all the immigrants. So many wonderful people from so many different parts of the world — if only there was a way we could join together and break free.

Wait a minute.

What if we didn't need one rich relative? What if what we needed instead was a lot of poor people? My mom said it herself — everybody could each put in a little.

Lupe came straight over the next day and squealed when I told her my plan.

"Of course! Why didn't we think of this earlier? Mr. Yao desperately wants to sell the motel. We could probably get it for cheap!"

She grabbed my hand and we ran out the

back to find Hank. It was a Saturday, and Hank was outside his room watering his tomato plant.

"How much do you think Mr. Yao wants for the motel?" we asked him.

Hank stopped watering and drew a sharp breath. "At least three hundred thousand dollars, I'd say. Why? Did you guys find another rich relative?"

No, we were all out of those. But we knew a lot of people. Sure, they were all poor, but if everybody put in a little . . .

"And it wouldn't be a donation. It'd be an investment! We'd own the motel together!" I told Hank. I pulled out my notebook and showed him and Lupe my calculations.

Their eyes boggled when they saw the math.

"This place makes twelve thousand dollars a month??" Lupe asked.

"Holy! That's *serious* money!" Hank exclaimed.

$144,000-a-year serious to be exact.

Hank slapped his leg.

"That's it, I'm in," he declared.

Hank emptied every pocket of every jacket. He dug his fingers into the backs of his chairs and checked under his bed for money. He even checked in his shoes. He managed to find $78.56, which wasn't a lot, but it was something. The other weeklies, as soon as they heard, wanted to contribute too. Fred put in $100, and Billy Bob put in $200. Mrs. T contributed $250, but it was Mrs. Q who put in the most, a whopping $3,000.

Hank whistled.

"You got three thousand dollars lying around and you're living in this dump?" he asked her. "Why don't you get an apartment?"

"This isn't a *dump,*" Mrs. Q said. "This is home! And besides, if I lived in an apartment, I'd never meet all of you wonderful people."

She gave my shoulder a squeeze.

Lupe skipped on home to talk to her parents. She said they had some sort of emergency fund, but she wasn't sure how much was in there.

As for me, I dug out my essay from the contest. I made copies of the essay and passed it out to every single customer who came in.

My plan was simple: find six hundred people to contribute $500 each. That would bring us to the grand total of $300,000. So far, we got $3,628 from the weeklies. We still had $296,371 to go.

A few customers threw my story in the trash, but a surprising number didn't. They responded with genuine interest and curiosity. A few were moved by what I told them about our situation and the kind of year we had been having and how we got through it by pulling together as a family. They opened up their checkbooks and wrote checks for $700, $1,000, $4,000, $5,000, and even $8,000.

One customer wanted to know my vision for the Calivista. His name was Mr. Cooper, and he was a venture capitalist from Los Angeles, passing through on his way down to San Diego. A venture capitalist, Mr. Cooper said, was someone who invested in small companies before they become big companies. Though he could afford to stay anywhere, Mr. Cooper still liked living frugally and that's why he was at the Calivista.

"Where do you see the Calivista in five years?" Mr. Cooper asked me.

"Right here," I said, a little confused by his question.

He laughed. "No, I mean, what kinds of things do you expect from the Calivista?"

I thought about it and said, "I just want everyone to be happy. Every single customer."

Mr. Cooper smiled. "That's the kind of vision I like to hear. I'd be honored to invest," he said.

Mr. Cooper took out his checkbook and wrote us a check for a jaw-dropping $50,000!

As he handed us the enormous check, my mother's hands shook. She'd never seen so many zeroes all in one place.

"I'm expecting big things from this place." Mr. Cooper beamed. "Big things!"

With Mr. Cooper's check and the other customers' contributions, we still needed about $230,000. So the next day, I went around to all the shops on our street. To my wild surprise, both Mr. Abayan from the convenience store and Mr. Bhagawati from the dry cleaners wanted to invest.

"Are you sure?" I asked them.

"Are you kidding? This is our chance to own a piece of land in America!" they said. They were tired of sending all their money back to their relatives month after month. For once, they were going to spend on themselves.

They gave me $1,000 each, cash. I ran all the way home clutching the thick stack of hundreds in my hands.

Lupe came over with even more thrilling news. Her parents talked it over and they wanted to invest $10,000, the entirety of their emergency fund.

"But it's your emergency fund!" I said. "Are you sure about this?"

Lupe nodded. "We've never been more sure of anything in our life," she said.

As her dad added his chunk to the huge pile of money, Lupe and I grabbed each other's arms and jumped up and down, screaming, "We're getting off the roller coaster! We're getting off the roller coaster!!"

By the end of the week, we were $85,000 down, $215,000 to go! I took out the big ledger and started writing to old customers. I wrote to Mr. Lewis, the guy who gave me a hard time about the key and wanted all those extra pillows. To my surprise, he wrote me back and sent me a check for $100 along with a gift certificate to Home Depot for a better key machine. Mr. and Mrs. Miller, the nice couple who gave me an eight-dollar tip, sent $75. They told their friend about it, a guy who made a fortune selling mops on the home shopping channel on TV, and he called us up and wanted to invest. My dad then got on the phone and started calling up some of the immigrants who had stayed at our motel. When the immigrants heard, they wanted to get in on the deal too.

Aunt Ling, Uncle Li, Uncle Fung, and

Uncle Zhu each invested $100, $125, $150, and $200. Even Uncle Zhang, who had just gotten a new job parking cars at a parking garage, put in $88, which pleased my parents very much because of the number eight.

Word got out that there was a killer investment opportunity, and soon immigrants all up and down the state were coming over to invest.

"If we can't have the American dream ourselves, maybe we can have it together!" the immigrants exclaimed.

My parents were in awe. They could not get over the fact that so many people — total strangers! — could believe in them like that, could look at them and decide, *Hey, I don't know you, but I believe in you. I believe in your dream.* And put crisp green bills into their tired, blistered hands. One stranger after another, flesh and bones that looked into their eyes and said yes, when time and time again, they looked at themselves and said no.

Two weeks later, an even more amazing thing happened.

Hank walked into the front office with a stack of bills. He slid the cash across the front desk, a thick stack of twenties.

"You found more money?" I asked.

"No. *You* found more money," he said.

I furrowed my eyebrows at him. I didn't understand.

"I got your money back from the essay people," he announced.

"You *what*?" I couldn't believe my ears. "How?"

"I took a page from your book," he said. "I wrote them a letter."

I reached over and touched the fresh green bills. My lucky penny money! I never thought I'd see it again.

"When I explained to them how young you are and how hard you worked for that money, they returned it like that." Hank snapped his fingers.

"Oh, Hank, thank you," I said.

He waved away my thanks like it was nothing, even though what he did meant the world to me.

"So what are you going to do with it?" Hank asked.

"I'll tell you what I'm going to do with it," I said. "I'm buying a motel with it!"

"That's my girl!" Hank beamed.

I wrote the Vermont people to say thank you for returning the money. That's when I had an idea.

Dear Vermont motel essay organizers,

Thank you so much for returning my entry fee. Can you do me a huge favor? Can you please kindly help me send the following letter out to all the other people who entered the essay contest but did not win? It would mean a lot to me.

Thank you.

Mia Tang

Letter attached:

Dear sir/madam,

My name is Mia Tang. I am ten years old and like you, I also entered the Vermont Motel Giveaway Essay Contest. For the past year, I have been helping my parents manage a motel in Anaheim, California. We have made it our home, from the towels we carefully fold each and every day to the customers we call family.

But you see, the motel is not ours. It belongs to a man named Mr. Yao, who is unkind and unjust and stubborn as a rock. My parents think that working for Mr. Yao is the only way but I don't think so. At night, I dreamed of a better way. I dreamed of owning a motel one day that was ours. So I entered the Vermont Motel Giveaway Essay Contest.

Sadly, though, I did not win. I always knew losing was a possibility. What are the chances of actually winning a motel? But, still, it hurt, watching my hopes and dreams disappear. You probably know the feeling.

Well, maybe all our hopes and dreams don't have to disappear. I am writing to you because something has happened here at the Calivista Motel. Mr. Yao is selling the motel! He's selling it for cheap because he's desperate. We're all chipping in to see if we can buy it from him and we're looking for investors. If you would like to invest, please let me know.

It wouldn't be a donation. You would be one of the owners and in the future, whenever a customer comes to stay at the Calivista, part of that money would go to you.

You might be asking yourself, why should I invest in a motel from a 10 year old? For three reasons:

1. I know what I'm doing. I know every corner of this motel like the back of my hand because I've lived here and worked here for almost a year.

2. I <u>love</u> what I'm doing. I'm very proud of my work. Every day, I check

people in at the front desk. The customers like me (see enclosed feedback cards) because I always go the extra mile for them.

3. I won't let you down. I will work hard every day for my dream and yours.

So what do you say?

If we can't win a motel, together, let's buy one! No investment is too small. Even if all you have are some extra pennies and nickels lying around, we'll take them (you'd be amazed what some of them are worth). I look forward to hearing from you.

Yours truly,
Mia Tang
Manager

A few weeks later, the checks started rolling in! The Vermont essay people sent my letter out and to my absolute amazement, people from all over the country sent in checks for $50, $100, $2,000, and even $10,000! By the end of that incredible month, and with everyone else's investments, we had reached $300,000! We cashed the checks at the bank and kept all the cash in a giant trash bag which my parents held in their arms at all times and slept with at night in case any robbers came.

CHAPTER 64

The nerves tingled in my toes as Mr. Yao's Lincoln Navigator pulled into the motel. We told him on the phone we had something very important to discuss with him.

"So? What's this all about?" he asked, plopping himself down on the couch.

Nervously, my mom looked at my dad. I glanced toward my room, where the trash bag of cash was, and out the small kitchen window where Hank's, Billy Bob's, and Mrs. Q's heads were squeezed together, trying to peer in. They all knew this was the big moment.

"We . . . we'd like to discuss buying the motel," my mom said.

Mr. Yao sat up.

"Why? Did an interested buyer come?" he asked.

My dad cleared his voice. "Yes," he said.

"Well, who is it?" Mr. Yao asked.

"Us," my dad said.

"You?" Mr. Yao said.

He started laughing.

"How much did you come up with? Five hundred dollars?" He chuckled.

"Actually, we came up with three hundred thousand dollars," my dad said.

Mr. Yao stopped laughing.

A war was happening in Mr. Yao's face as denial morphed into rage.

"How the heck did *you* get three hundred thousand dollars?" Mr. Yao finally asked.

"That's not important," my dad said. "What's important is, do we have a deal or not?"

Again, Mr. Yao burst out laughing.

"Do we have a deal or not? Who do you think you are?"

I jumped in.

"He's a guy who's about to buy your motel, that's who he is!" I told him.

"Oh, no, he's not," Mr. Yao snapped. "There's another buyer interested. And he's offering more."

"How much more?"

Mr. Yao shrugged.

"How much?" my dad repeated.

"What's the difference? You can't afford it."

"How much?"

"Fifty thousand."

■ ■ ■ ■

We called up every single investor, but unfortunately, nobody had any extra money. They had already given us every dollar they had. Even Mr. Cooper said his hands were tied. He added that if the deal did not go through by the end of the month, he would need his $50,000 back so he could put it into one of his other investments.

I dropped my head into my hands. Everything was slipping away, all my hard work. It felt like losing the essay contest all over again, except it hurt so much more because this time I was letting *everyone* down.

I hugged the humongous trash bag of money and cried. I cried for all the motel essay contest applicants, who once again, failed to get a motel. I cried for young Hank, getting pushed around by all those mean kids, and old Hank, forty years later, still getting treated unfairly, and for Lupe's dad, boiling away on the roof every single day under the blistering sun. I cried for Mr. Abayan, the convenience store guy from the Philippines, and Mr. Bhagawati, the laundry guy, with his raisiny fingers and hunched back washing bundle after bundle of clothes. I cried for Uncle Zhang, poor Uncle Zhang, who had no money but still insisted on contributing because it was so important to him to help us in our hour of need. And all the other uncles and aunts who sent us money, hoping for a slice, however tiny, of the American dream.

And now it was all going to fall apart over $50,000 — $50,000 we couldn't come up with, even if you opened us up and sold us for parts.

Slowly, I stood. I dried my tears, picked up the bag of money, and walked into the living room.

"Hey, where are you going with that?" my parents asked me.

"I'm going to call the investors. Start returning all of this money," I told my parents.

They shook their heads.

"We have an idea," they said.

CHAPTER 65

"No," I said, shaking my head firmly.

"Just this once," my dad said. "We're so close."

"Dad! You saw what happened to Uncle Ming!"

The memory of his black eye and the bruises on his neck where the loan sharks grabbed him ripped through me.

"I know. But this is different. You said it yourself, this is a huge opportunity."

I looked up at my dad. I had never seen so much determination and hope in his eyes.

"We're *this* close," my dad said, holding up his fingers.

My mother put her hand over mine.

"Just this once," she repeated. "We'll pay them right back. Just this once."

Hour after terrifying hour, I sat and waited at the front desk. The loan sharks were coming. I pictured hammerheads swimming up to the front desk, glaring at us from the sides of their heads.

They pulled into the motel in a black Cadillac DeVille. Three big Chinese guys stepped out. They were all wearing leather jackets. One of them had a tattoo of the word *ren* in Chinese on his neck, which means "to suffer." Another had a big tear in his ear, like someone had ripped out his earring. And the third, the boss of the group, had oily skin and long stringy hair, which he wore in a ponytail. There was a great big bulge in his jacket and I swallowed hard as they stepped through the bulletproof glass door.

"You understand for an amount this large, we're going to need some collateral," the oily boss of the loan sharks said to my dad.

The three of them sat on the small sofa in our living room. With a trembling hand, my mom poured them the last of our jasmine tea.

"Yes," my dad said. "That makes sense. What do you need?"

"Passport, ID," he said.

I felt myself go cold.

"But Uncle Zhang!" I reminded my dad. My dad put a finger over his mouth. *Not now. . . .*

"It'll be returned to you, of course, when you pay us back," the oily boss said.

His voice lingered.

"But if you *don't* pay us back the fifty thousand dollars plus another twenty thousand on top, well, then . . ." The boss glanced at his associates.

His associates stretched out their hands and cracked their knuckles.

With every crack, fear jolted down my spine.

CHAPTER 66

It was decided that the next afternoon, the loan sharks would come back with the $50,000 and my parents would hand over our passports and IDs. I walked to school with nails in my stomach.

It was the last day of school. As we all cleaned out our desks and counted down to the last hour, Jason walked up to me.

"Hey," he said.

In his hand, he was holding a pencil. It was my sparkly green pencil!

"Been meaning to give this back to you," he said, handing the pencil to me.

I looked down at the pencil in my hands. I'd expected it to be super short and beat-up by now — I had had visions of Jason's dog chewing on it, Jason stabbing things at home with it, wearing it down to a nub — but it was exactly the same length as before and as beautiful and sparkly as ever.

"Thank you," I said. "This means a lot to

me." I hugged my pencil in my hands.

"I'm sure you'll write great things with it," he added. I looked up at him, surprised. "Like the piece you wrote about coming to America."

A smile stretched across my face.

"Thanks," I said.

Jason looked down at the floor. "I'm sorry I made your year so miserable," he said softly.

"It's okay," I said. "I'm sorry too for . . . you know."

I could see in his eyes I did not need to remind him about the time in the auditorium. He probably remembered every day.

"Here. I have something for you too," I said. I reached deep into my backpack and pulled out the thank-you letter I'd been meaning to give him. I'd been carrying it around in my backpack for months.

Jason looked down at the note, surprised.

He smiled as he read my words.

As I turned to leave, Jason reached out and touched my arm.

"What?" I asked.

"He's bluffing. There's no other buyer. It's just you guys. He'll take a lot less for the motel."

I stared at Jason. His brown eyes blazed with courage.

But it was his kindness that blew me away. When the school bell rang, I ran.

CHAPTER 67

I ran as fast as the wind could carry me, adrenaline powering my skinny little legs. With each step, I whispered a prayer. *Please. Let me get there before the loan sharks do.*

I turned the corner onto Coast Boulevard just as the loan sharks' Cadillac pulled into the motel.

As the three loan sharks got out of their car with their suitcases full of cash, I raced into the parking lot screaming, "Mom! Dad! Don't do it! Mr. Yao's bluffing!"

My parents promptly called the deal off. The loan sharks grumbled about how they came all this way and went to a great deal of effort to put the money together, so my dad gave them twenty dollars for the gas and their troubles, and they piled back into their car and left.

As they drove away, my parents collapsed onto the ground.

"That was close!" my mother exclaimed.

My dad put his hand over his pounding heart as he stared at the wide-open sky.

"Thank God," my dad said.

As my parents lay panting on the side of the parking lot, I walked over to the front desk and called Mr. Yao.

"Mr. Yao? We'd like to make an offer on the motel," I said. "Three hundred thousand dollars and not a penny more."

"He said yes!" I screamed, running through the motel.

The weeklies were in Hank's room playing Monopoly. When they heard the news that Mr. Yao agreed to sell to us, Hank slapped the Monopoly board and all the pieces went flying.

"What'd I tell you?" Hank said to Billy Bob. "If it can happen in Monopoly, it can happen in life!"

Mr. Yao came over with Jason and his real estate agent the next day, as did Lupe, Lupe's dad, Mr. Cooper, the immigrants, Mr. Abayan from the convenience store, Mr. Bhagawati from the Laundromat, and some of the motel essay people who had driven down because they wanted to see their new motel with their very own eyes. Mr. Cooper brought over his lawyer friend who helped us draw up the contract. There were so many people, we couldn't all fit in the manager's quarters. We had to put chairs and tables out in the parking lot.

"All right, let's get this over with," Mr. Yao said.

It took ages for Mr. Yao and his agent to count up all the money. When he was finally convinced it was all there, Mr. Yao lugged the bag over to his car and dumped it in the trunk.

His agent then sat down with Mr. Cooper's lawyer and pored over the sales and purchase agreement. We all huddled around them, watching as they wrote in each of our names under *Buyer.* There were so many owners, we needed three additional pages just to fill out all our names!

My father's voice shook as he told the agent how to spell his name.

"I never thought this day would actually happen," he said.

"Me neither, my friend," said Hank, putting an arm around my dad's shoulder. "Me neither."

When everyone finished signing their names and Mr. Yao officially handed my parents the keys, Lupe and I jumped up and down, screaming, "We did it! We did it! We did it!"

Jason smiled.

"You know what I'm going to do?" Hank asked, his eyes twinkling.

"What?" I asked.

Hank ran toward the sparkling blue pool. He let out a yelp as he jumped in fully clothed.

"Hey!" Mr. Yao called, but only with a fraction of his usual force. "You can't jump into my pool with your clothes on!"

"It's not your pool anymore!" Hank called back.

Mr. Yao opened his mouth to protest, then closed it.

One by one, Lupe and all the weeklies and essay people and immigrants jumped in too. My dad threw my mom in, and my mom shrieked with glee. Everyone was waiting for me to come in.

I turned to Jason.

"You coming?" I asked him.

Jason turned to his dad and asked if he could stay.

Mr. Yao scoffed.

"You don't want to go swimming with these losers, do you?" he asked his son.

Jason shook his head.

"No, Dad," he said. "I'm going swimming with the winners."

Hand in hand, we jumped into the pool.

As we splashed and swam in the sun-kissed water, my mother suddenly remembered something very important.

"Wait, wait, wait!" she said. "Let's get a picture!"

"I'll take it!" Hank jumped out. As he held his hand up and clicked, I looked around at my new family and smiled.

It was a picture I'd been waiting a long, long time for.

AUTHOR'S NOTE

Many of the events in *Front Desk* are based on reality. Growing up, I helped my parents manage several motels in California from when I was eight years old to when I was twelve years old.

As a kid, I both loved and feared the front desk. I loved the thrill of working, the fact

that I could ask an adult for their ID and they'd have to give it to me. I was also petrified at night. I would go to sleep with this choking, painful anxiety, not knowing what might happen in the middle of the night. (The part about Mia's mom getting beaten up really happened to my own mother.) Would both my parents still be there in the morning when I woke up?

At school, I couldn't talk about it with any of my friends. How could I explain to them that my parents came to the United States with only $200 in their pocket? That for the first year, I slept on a mattress we pulled out of the Dumpster, hoping my dreams greeted me before the stench did.

I also couldn't explain the love and hope that grew out of poverty. How much I bonded with the weeklies. How we watched out for one another and celebrated the joys together, however small. How my parents hid fellow immigrants from the boss (and used a blue baseball cap on the front desk as the secret sign!). How a pair of stray cats had kittens on the back stairwell and we hid the kittens in the rooms too. How my dad made soup for the customers when they weren't feeling well.

How we became a family.

Our new family helped us get through the loneliness and frustration of our situation, the fact that we left behind our friends and family in China, thinking we were going to a better land, only to see our friends and family get rich back home in a way no one could have ever foreseen.

There were 536,000 immigrants from mainland China living in the United States in 1990.[1] Unlike the Chinese immigrants who came before them, the post-1965 Chinese immigrants were predominately

1. "Chinese Immigrants in the United States," Migration Policy Institute, last modified January 28, 2015, http://www.migrationpolicy.org/article/chinese-immigrants-united-states.

skilled. They were highly educated, leaving behind good careers. They took a bet that China was not going to change. They were wrong.

Many of them left with very little money because China was still fairly communist in the '80s and early '90s. China has, of course, modernized greatly since then. There is no longer the one child policy (now there's the two child policy) and apartments in Beijing and Shanghai now cost several million US dollars (and come with private showers!). But in 1990, China's per capita GDP was only US$317.[2] Once in the United States, these immigrants struggled to survive, working long, excruciating hours in manual labor jobs for very little pay. The median annual income in 1989 for Chinese immigrants in the United States was only $8,000 — lower than that of any other immigrant group.[3]

This unique set of circumstances made

2. "GDP per capita," The World Bank, http://data .worldbank.org/indicator/NY.GDP.PCAP.CD ?end=2015&page=6&start=1990.
3. "Research on Immigrant Earnings," Social Security Administration, last modified August 2008, https://www.ssa.gov/policy/docs/ssb/v68n1/ v68n1p31-text.html#chart2.

these immigrants particularly vulnerable to exploitation and hardship. No group of Chinese immigrants before or since came with quite so little and gave up quite so much.

Later, some of these immigrants would go back to China and not recognize the country they left. They would not recognize their brothers and sisters, in their designer clothes and handbags. Their brothers and sisters would not recognize them. Neither would the new Chinese immigrants, who would arrive in business class and not understand why anybody would ever turn to the loan sharks.

I grew up listening to the stories of these immigrants, stories that brought tears to my eyes and chilled the air in my lungs. I'll never forget when my mom's friend came to stay with us and confessed he worked eighteen-hour days and slept in his boss's basement because his boss took away his passport and ID. I stayed up all night writing his boss a letter. Though I was just a kid, my letter scared the boss and my mom's friend was freed.

I hope in telling these stories, these immigrants' struggles and sacrifices will not be forgotten. *They* will not be forgotten.

And to the nearly twenty million immigrant children currently living in the United States (30 percent of whom are living at or below poverty),[4] I hope this book brings some comfort and hope. You are not alone. Somewhere out there, someone in the universe understands exactly what you're going through, including all the fears swirling in your mind or your parents' minds that you're just a bike. You are NOT a bike.

Finally, I hope that through this book, more people will understand the importance of tolerance and diversity. The owner of one of the motels we managed told us not to rent to African Americans, saying they were dangerous. This infuriated us, and we did not listen. To this day, my family and I are forever grateful to the many, many wonderful people from all different backgrounds who made us feel welcome in our new country and helped us in times of need.

Often during tough times, the first instinct is to exclude. But this book is about what happens when you include, when, despite all your suffering and your heartache, you

4. "DataBank: Immigrant Children, Appendix 2," Child Trends, last modified October 2014, https://www.childtrends.org/wp-content/uploads/2012/07/110_appendix2.pdf.

still wake up every morning and look out at the world with fresh, curious eyes.

ACKNOWLEDGMENTS

Writing a book can be a lonely experience. For so many weeks, it's just you and the manuscript. You withdraw into yourself, comforted and entertained by words not uttered by actual people but the sole product of your imagination. You stay this way for quite a while, enjoying this most delicious secret. Until one day, you decide, it is time.

When I decided it was time with *Front Desk,* I had no idea what the reaction would be. Questions and doubt flooded my mind, just like Mia's mind, questions like "Am I good enough?" and "Will anybody really care about my story?" The answer came in the form of a resounding YES from my agent, Alex Slater. Opening your email was one of the best days of my life. Alex, you are the reason *Front Desk* is not just another random file on my computer. Thank you for believing in me. Thank you for believing in this book since day one and fighting tooth and nail to bring it to the world.

To my brilliant editor, Nick Thomas, thank you for pushing me with each draft. Thank you for *getting* this story and, more importantly, knowing how to make it better. In music, there are people who can listen to a freshly composed song once and immediately know what two notes would make the song *amazing.* That's what you do for manuscripts. Thanks for giving me those notes.

To my publisher, Arthur Levine, thank you for welcoming me to the AALB family. I could not have found a more dedicated or loving home. To the greater Scholastic team — Rachel Gluckstern, Tracy van Straaten, Lizette Serrano, Rachel Feld, Vaishali Nayak — thank you for supporting *Front Desk*. It's such an honor to be a Scholastic author, and I pinch myself every day.

To Cheryl Klein, who picked up the book when it was a silly, slapstick story with a couple of moving scenes thrown in and saw the potential. I hope you're pleased with the final product. You are *Front Desk*'s angel.

To my dear friend Fran Lebowitz, my cheerleader and shoulder to cry on — thank you for reading *Front Desk* when it was still in its infancy. With every new draft, I heard your voice in my head: "DIG DEEPER." I hope the final draft is deep enough for you ;-).

To my editor at the *South China Morning Post* and friend, Rob Haddow, thanks for all your friendship and guidance over the years. You believed in me when I was a young, unknown writer and patiently guided me with each column. From the bottom of my heart, thank you.

To my professor from college Bruce Cain, thank you for mentoring me from a young age and teaching me, among many other things, the importance of always meeting deadlines. Many thanks to early readers Bonni Lee, Fiona Kotur Marin, and my dear friend and mentor Paul Cummins, whose wisdom, generosity, and passion for education inspire me every day. Your friendship has meant so much to me. Thanks as well to Peter Gordon for all your advice over the years. And to my professors Terri Bimes and Eric Schickler, who instilled in me a love of research (and road trips).

To my good friend and esteemed criminal defense attorney Javier Damien, thank you for advising me on the scenes involving criminal law! You're the best! Thanks as well to Yanelli Guerrero for your help and insight on the character of Lupe and life in Mexico! My sincere thanks to Bri Webber for your thoughtful comments on Hank — they were super helpful!

A huge thank-you to the incredible team at Trident — Nicola DeRobertis-Theye, Sara Pearl, Erica Spellman-Silverman — you guys are amazing!!! Thanks for championing *Front Desk*! Your support means so much to me!

Thank you to my colleagues at The Kelly Yang Project, in particular Paul Smith and Queenie Chu. It's an honor and privilege working with you. To all my students and the greater KYP community, thank you for believing in me and inspiring me with your joy and wonder. As a teacher, I loved writing all the classroom scenes.

To my own teachers from elementary school, Mrs. Faast, Mr. Vaiuso, Mrs. Smith, Mrs. Bailey, Mrs. Hanchey, Mrs. Gallien, Mrs. McDonald, thank you for encouraging me to keep writing. To the wonderful librarians all over America — I am where I am today because of you. I still remember being eight years old, living in the motels, wondering if I would ever get out of there. You gave me wings to fly. Those wings came in the form of books.

Last but not least, to my family.

To my mom and dad, who came to America and sacrificed so much so that I might have a better life. Thanks for letting me man the front desk when I was a kid. I hope to God *Front Desk* gets translated so you guys can read it. Thank you, Mom, for helping me take care of my kids now so I can write. You guys are amazing.

To my husband, thank you for all the chicken dinners ☺. Thank you for drilling into me not to use a cliché. Most of all, thanks for going on this crazy journey with me. I'm grateful I have you in my corner.

To my muffin, banana bread, and sourdough, I LOVE YOU GUYS!!! I first wrote this story in the summer of 2015 for my oldest son, Eliot. Every day, I wrote a chapter and we would read that chapter together. Toward the end of that summer, Eliot went away to camp for a few weeks. I thought for sure he'd forget all about *Front Desk.* Thanks for not forgetting and encouraging mommy to do something with my story. You three are my world. I love you to the moon and back.

Finally, to all the aunts and uncles who shared their stories with me and my family when I was growing up — thank you, and I hope I did your stories justice.

ABOUT THE AUTHOR

Kelly Yang's family immigrated from China when she was a young girl, and she grew up in California, in circumstances very similar to those of Mia Tang. She eventually left the motels and went to college at the age of thirteen, and is a graduate of UC Berkeley and Harvard Law School. She was one of the youngest women to graduate from Harvard Law School. Upon graduation, she gave up law to pursue her dream of writing and teaching kids writing. She is the founder of The Kelly Yang Project, a leading writing and debating program for children in Asia and the United States. She is also a columnist for the *South China Morning Post* and has been published in the *New York Times,* the *Washington Post,* and the *Atlantic.* Kelly is the mother of three children and splits her time between Hong Kong and San Francisco. Please find her online at:

www.kellyyang.com
Twitter: @kellyyanghk
Youtube:
www.youtube.com/kellyyangproject
Instagram: kellyyanghk
Facebook:
www.facebook.com/kellyyangproject